FAITH BASED DIPLOMACY

The Challenge To Development

by
John Chikago

authorHOUSE™

1663 LIBERTY DRIVE, SUITE 200
BLOOMINGTON, INDIANA 47403
(800) 839-8640
WWW.AUTHORHOUSE.COM

First published by AuthorHouse 01/12/05

ISBN: 1-4208-2560-7 (e)
ISBN: 1-4208-2558-5 (sc)
ISBN: 1-4208-2559-3 (dj)

Printed in the United States of America
Bloomington, Indiana

This book is printed on acid-free paper.

<u>PRAYER</u>

Dear Heavenly Father,

Thank you that you are indeed the Creator of the universe, the Creator of Earth, and thank you that you created man and woman in Your own image.

Thank you, Dear Lord, that according to the Bible you sent our Lord Jesus Christ as the image of the invisible God, to be a perfect sacrifice for each of us, so our sins may be fully and completely forgiven, and that by faith, those who believe in You and call You Lord, will receive eternal salvation and the Hope that is beyond human understanding.

And thank you, Heavenly Father for the vision that you have given for the publishing of this book, entitled FAITH BASED DIPLOMACY - The Challenge To Development, *so that everyone in developing countries of the world may place hope in Christ before placing it in political systems or in man-made solutions to life's problems. Lord, I pray that all born again Christians will be thankful and hopeful because you have called each of us by Your Name to be ambassadors of the Hope that is in Christ Jesus.*

Romans 8:24 reminds us that "In the Hope of Christ we were saved. Hope that is seen is no hope at all. Who hopes for what he already has? But if we hope for what we do not yet have, we wait for it patiently." Lord, I pray that the readers of this book will faithfully place their hope in You and not in things that are here today and gone tomorrow…but in You…who is the Alpha and the Omega…the Beginning and the End.

In Jesus Name, Amen!

Dennis Folds
Senior Pastor
Tokyo Baptist Church (International)

MAP OF MALAWI

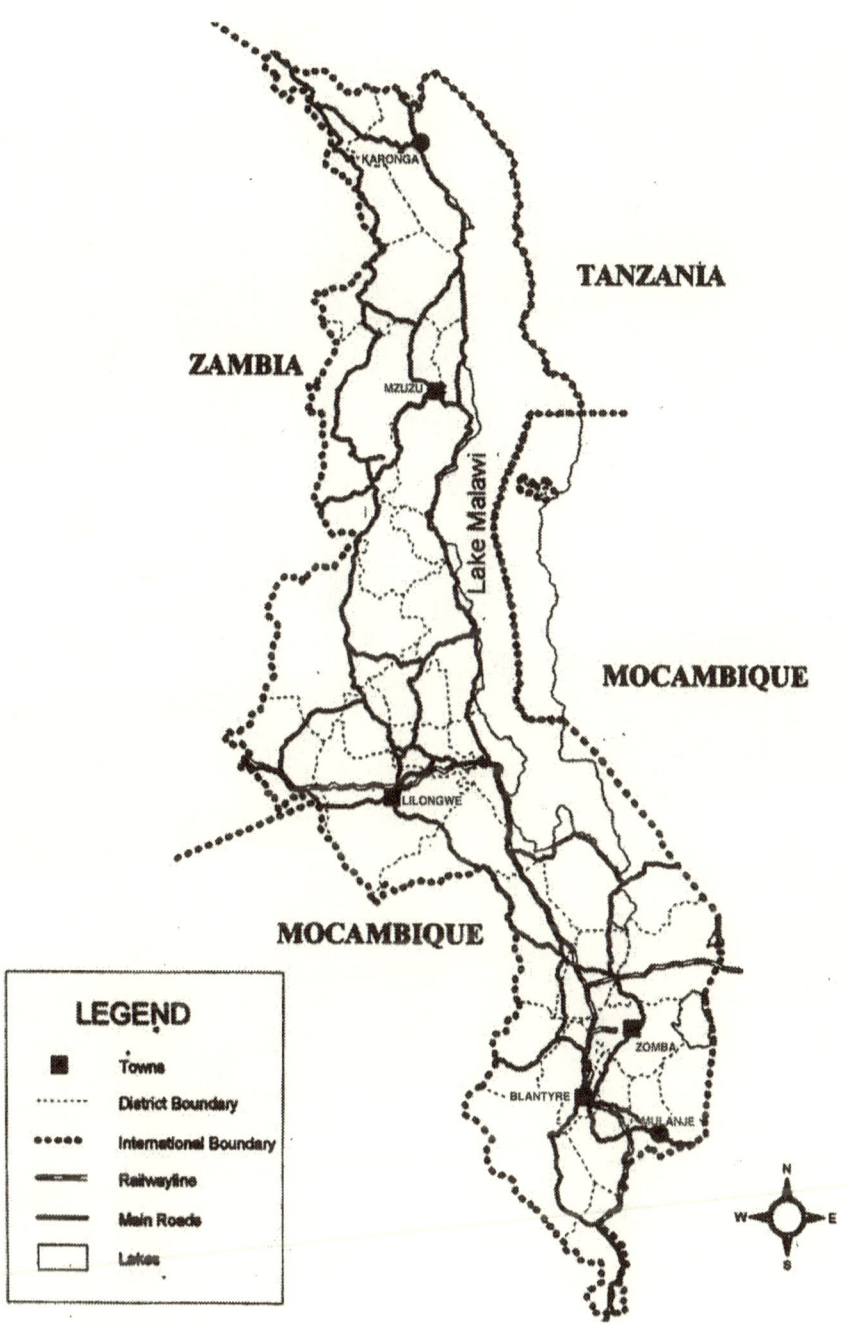

TABLE OF CONTENTS

ACKNOWLEDGEMENTS

Publishing *FAITH BASED DIPLOMACY - The Challenge To Development* demanded the involvement of many organizations and individuals. It is to those individuals and organizations that I am deeply indebted. I am most grateful to the government and people of Malawi for the privilege of my appointment to the diplomatic service. This is a great privilege to my family and me personally.

Admittedly my time in the diplomatic service has accorded me the rare privilege of understanding what it means to serve others as required of Christian believers. As a born-again Christian, I feel greatly honored by this practical realization.

I must also admit that the opportunity of the appointment has enabled me to gain good understanding of contemporary global issues. I am therefore full of appreciation for the support I have received from many friends and colleagues when discussing this book. I am particularly grateful to my trusted neighbor from the country of the Republic of Tanzania, His Excellency Mr. E. E. E. Mtango, that country's Ambassador to Japan. I have always cherished his brotherly pieces of advice. His contributions and ideas when discussing this book were very helpful. Also, I cannot forget my many Japanese friends including Ambassador Y. Kurokochi who graciously agreed to review the manuscript and write its foreword. They have all been supportive of my ideas of publishing this book.

I must also thank Pastor Dennis Folds, Senior Pastor at the Tokyo Baptist Church, for his prayer. The prayer helped me to meet the objectives of the book. I believe that it is only through faith in our Lord Jesus Christ that the problems being faced in developing countries will be resolved one by one.

We must never forget that God created every country and its natural resources, thereby enabling each country to pursue its own economic plans. Therefore, any national economic plan which does not recognize the economic plan made by God is doomed to fail.

The production of the manuscript and its subsequent readings were the most trying to the members of my family. I wish to loudly thank my wife Margaret for her patience. My son Dick deserves thanks for his advice on the quality and choice of the American publisher. He also worked closely with the publisher in spite of his busy schedules. As always, I am also grateful to my two daughters Edith and Agnes, who lifted my morale throughout the process of writing the manuscript.

This is my second book after publishing _Crossing Cultural Frontiers_. No doubt, the members of my family may be thinking that book writing is now becoming my best partner. I also wish to thank Memory and Nick my adopted children for their indulgence when the need arose for their assistance in the production and checking of the manuscript.

I am most grateful to God for giving me the energy to think through and publish the book. At one point I fell sick; my worry was on nothing but the completion of this manuscript. I prayed to the Lord to restore my energy, and He did within just one week. In short, this book is the culmination of many positive efforts. I want to thank Makino-san my Secretary for her background support and Tamaki-san for her assistance.

FAITH BASED DIPLOMACY - The Challenge To Development is expected to be useful to everyone. Students of diplomacy and international relations will find it to be good reading material. Politicians making diplomatic policy decisions should find it helpful for preparing debates in parliaments.

Bureaucrats implementing policies for Foreign Service will also find it extremely instructive. Serving diplomats will find it refreshing. There is no doubt that when reading it, some will discover a plethora of ideas. When they do, the purposes for publishing the book will be achieved.

I hope you will enjoy reading *FAITH BASED DIPLOMACY - The Challenge To Development*. It has been written with the aim of offering encouragements and moral support to those people experiencing economic hardships in developing countries. It does not offer prescriptions as much as a new way of looking at problems. Unless those experiencing the problems accept that God created them after creating the universe, and that God had a reason for doing that, the situation will not change. It will be business as usual with positive efforts wasted on political systems and man-made solutions.

James John Chikago
TOKYO
September, 2004

FOREWORD

It is a distinct honor and privilege for me to write the foreword to this book by His Excellency Ambassador James John Chikago, the present Ambassador of the Republic of Malawi to Japan. I would like to say that this work by Ambassador Chikago in many respects is a unique and illuminating book on diplomacy and diplomatic life.

One usually associates diplomacy with a tight-lipped approach. Some diplomats do write memoirs after retirement, cataloguing outstanding diplomatic feats in which they participated. But Ambassador Chikago is in active service. He writes about "development diplomacy" with real enthusiasm, openly supporting the idea of making diplomacy more transparent so that it will be openly discussed and supported by the people, particularly those citizens of a developing country where achieving economic development is a paramount objective.

I know of no book on diplomacy by an African ambassador, whether in retirement or in active service, which attempts to explain and foster a sense of participation in diplomacy.

As a former businessman in Malawi, Ambassador Chikago approaches diplomacy with a businessman's point of view and succeeds in giving new revelations on how and how not to conduct diplomacy for the development of a country. Many points he addresses are very urgent and valid, and I have no objection to that; however, I permit myself to say that diplomacy has its own peculiarities distinguishable from business management.

Diplomacy is sometimes associated with balls, banquets and other prestigious events of pomp and splendor. While sometimes true, I am constrained to note that diplomacy involves much repetition and day-to-day drudgery. Those dreaming of pageants and grand splendour should stay away from diplomacy, because this is not the diplomacy needed by the developing world.

The tasks diplomats do and work to accomplish are not known entirely by the public. Some diplomatic achievements, even if spectacular, better remain unknown. And diplomats do remain tight-lipped, even when elated over their successes. For example, if one speaks of one's "tremendous success" which may place one's counterparts in an unfavourable light, or invite blame of "failure" on them, one is not a diplomat in the true sense of the word. While journalists may lionize a diplomat for one's political feat, one had better take a self-effacing attitude and choose oblivion. Diplomatic history abounds in instances of veritable success not known as such, and the participating diplomats should only take delight in receiving kudos posthumously, if at all.

Regarding good diplomats, each country has its set of values and cultural traditions to be inculcated in up-and-coming diplomats. Cross-cultural contacts at overseas postings enrich them but, without sufficient pre-departure training, diplomats may proceed to their posts with limited sensitivity vis-à-vis foreign culture. Diplomats must be accessible at overseas posts to people and foreigners as mirrors reflecting the best images of their own country, while introducing conversely respectable facades of the country of assignment and its people to their own countrymen. Diplomats engage in wide-ranging activities, sometimes in unfriendly climatic conditions, while facing the difficult-to-crack mindset of people.

Diplomats have their individual aptitudes. They may play golf, bridge, chess, or be ballroom dancing experts of international standard. Such people may possess special keys to an unknown network of people who willingly facilitate their activities. Conversely, there may be those who work fervently with local charitable activities such as assisting the handicapped. Most importantly they must have a direct feel of the society and country in which they work.

Ideally, diplomats should take up their assignments together with their family members. Their wives (or husbands) and children can oftentimes serve as conveyors or breeders of friendship oftentimes more effectively and expansively than the diplomats themselves. The citizens of the diplomats-assigned country form opinions, often favorable, of the diplomats' homeland by their families' behavior, stories and reports.

The list of the different aspects of diplomatic life can be endless, but this is not the right place to go further. In this book Ambassador Chikago focuses on "development diplomacy", not development of diplomacy. Development diplomacy is a new term to many people; the contents as well as the methods are still being expanded. It is my ardent hope that Ambassador Chikago's book will lead the discussions toward fruitful formulation of a fertile system of development diplomacy.

Yasushi Kurokochi
Ambassador (Rtd)
September 2004

INTRODUCTION

The scriptures say that in the beginning, God created the Heavens and the Earth. Later, God created man in His image with authority over fish, birds, livestock, and everything, including all creatures that move on the ground. In this respect, it means there is nothing that exists without God's plans. God has plans for every living creature, every country, every nation, every person and every government. Diplomatic missions are no exception. Although diplomatic missions have historical connections, it is God who controls them.

I am aware there are already many books on diplomacy on the market. It is therefore appropriate to ask what the book *FAITH BASED DIPLOMACY - The Challenge To Development* is expected to achieve. It is fashionable for book publishers to follow market demands, commonly known as the market-driven approach. The approach adopted for this book is diametrically opposite to established market principles. The difference between this book and others is that it is based on Christian faith. Having worked in the private sector before, I have concluded that diplomacy is not treated as part of God's work. When talking about diplomacy, many do so without understanding what they are talking about. The concept that one draws a map of a mountain after leaving its peak and going to the lowland is relevant.

Unlike other books, *FAITH BASED DIPLOMACY - The Challenge To Development* is based on faith in the scriptures and practical management experiences. It is not a theoretical treatise that has attracted the interest of many writers. Therefore, the arguments advanced in the book are practical. Indeed the book delves into uncharted territory, focusing on the implementation of development diplomacy inspired by the Christian faith.

This book will very likely have a mixed reception. It is important to say from the outset that the book does not reflect the opinion or management of any specific diplomatic mission. The issues raised in the book cut across the whole diplomatic "industry." Most of the information used has been extracted from the work of academic research conducted in 2000. When there are disagreements on the content, the objectives of the book will have been achieved. Others will welcome the book for providing insights into a closed profession. With this presumption, there is optimism that the book has delved into a subject that has attracted exceptional public interest among citizens in developing countries. The enduring question by citizens is value for money from diplomacy.

Traditionally, diplomacy has not been a subject for ordinary people. In spite of being the largest conduit for public funds, the activities of diplomatic missions have been conducted in secrecy. Every time there is an attempt to discuss the role of diplomacy, the precondition has been confidentiality. It is not being disrespectful to say that for far too long the diplomacy has been shrouded in secrecy, almost bordering on intelligence gathering. No doubt it is because of this state of affairs that citizens in developing countries have been overwhelmed by confusion, compounded a misinterpretation of what diplomacy is.

One would think the knowledge deficiency has been caused by the inability of writers to treat diplomacy as a management subject. The situation defeats the established management principle that demands correlation between importance and degree of control. The degree of control to any activity should be relative to its importance. It requires the existence of positive correlation between value of the activity and degree of control. The implication is that any control action should be relative; therefore, it is not right for management writers to continue viewing diplomacy as an alien subject.

In light of the preceding observations, this book is expected to fill a strategic gap. This is the purpose for which it has been published. Its publication is under the presumption that management is generic. There should be no exceptions to the treatment of diplomacy. The differences arising from the nature of work undertaken at the diplomatic missions should not be justification. The common factor is that the diplomatic missions are public offices just like any other public office. Given a choice, the money spent on running the diplomatic missions should have been allocated to the social sectors. After all, addressing structural problems in the social sectors offers better returns to politicians than maintaining diplomatic missions.

The improvement of management practices at diplomatic missions cannot be achieved in the absence of faith-based values. The first precondition for resource utilization efficiency is love for one another. In the Great Commandment, Jesus Christ explains that love of God and love of others are the two most important laws to be observed by believers. When people do not have love for one another, they become selfish. This is the root cause of corruption. Improved public service delivery is achieved though high resource productivity. National productivity improvement is a collective effort in which all the citizens have to be involved. Therefore, without love for one another there cannot be community spirit.

The introduction of democracy in most developing countries has enabled ordinary citizens to demand information on public service delivery. It has become their basic right to know the contributions made by public offices. Obviously, the citizens want to see value for their money. There are some citizens inevitably confused by the process of privatization. Such people believe that diplomatic missions work as marketing houses in foreign countries, operating in much the same way as trade commissions. The presumption is that diplomatic missions should be driven by the private sector. Their confusion is understandable due to the absence of books on management. The dictatorial regimes did not allow the people to question government practices. Consequently, the citizens relied on half truths. Those who had correct pieces of information were the privileged ones within the ruling clique. Those who did not were treated as passive recipients of public policy. It is up to each nation's government to provide adequate public information. It is counterproductive to mistake public curiosity as enemy force. The people are not enemies, but friends of democracy.

The citizens want to know the purpose for the continued operation of diplomatic missions. The general impression is that diplomatic missions waste taxpayers' money that should have been used to improve deteriorating public services. In sensitivity to public outcry, some developing countries are now promoting *development diplomacy*. To most of the countries, the change to development diplomacy is a panacea.

It is wrong to assume that the change to development diplomacy is a new development. The pursuit of development diplomacy has always been the preoccupation of developed countries. In fact the rapid spread of imperialism and colonialism was driven by development diplomacy. Consequently, it was only the developing countries which were pursuing the diplomacy of friendship. As Breslin [2002.

p.61] confirms, diplomacy in Byzantine Constantinople focused on the promotion of economic interests, in particular those associated with the control of strategic sea routes.

FAITH BASED DILOMACY - The Challenge To Development has ten provocative chapters, covering subjects such as rethinking prevailing management practices at diplomatic missions; alternative ways to manage diplomatic missions; establishing networks at diplomatic missions consistent with the Great Commission where the Lord Jesus Christ commanded his followers to go out and make disciples, and the Japanese government's introduction of the Tokyo International Conference on Africa Development process (TICAD) in 1993; implying that the concept of development diplomacy is also a Japanese initiative, and the importance of effective time management and efficiency by governments working to successfully implement development diplomacy."

Finally, this book distinguishes itself from others in two ways. First, it is based on practical experience. Second, it is influenced by faith. It looks at the innovation of development diplomacy and how, if not implemented properly, it could be worsen the misery of developing countries.

It is the author's expectation that this book will be useful to a cross-section of people – as a useful reference to popularly elected officials; educational to newly appointed Foreign Service officers; and helpful to bureaucrats when making important management decisions affecting the Foreign Service. In short, it is the author's hope that it will be a useful book for everyone, irrespective of their status.

PRELUDE

During the period from June 1998 to December 2000, I conducted an academic research, investigating performance management at embassies. My research was conducted in two phases.

The first phase dealt with staff management, particularly recruitment, remuneration and control. Staff management was considered in regards to its significant impact on overall expenditure; specifically, the involvement of foreign exchange transactions.

The research findings showed a major weakness of staff performance monitoring systems. The imperatives of classical bureaucracy inhibited staff performance as control was separated from the point of action, proving that no effective control could be exercised in the absence of purpose statements, operating objectives, and performance targets.

The second phase of the research focused on financial control systems. The findings showed that embassies, in spite of assuming new mandates after the demise of the Cold War in 1991, continued to operate as delivery pipes for domestic policies primed by the political systems.

This out-of-balance condition was the notable disparity between policy and expectation. The power of faith was not part of the embassy culture. Traditionally the public sector perceived faith as a personal basic right; but without placing hope in the invisible power of God, nothing could be achieved.

The change of policy mandates in 1991 was an effect, not the cause. Naturally, the appropriate systems, structures, strategies and superordinate goals intended to support the new policy mandates are still evolving. This is why the Tokyo International Conference on African Development (TICAD) process initiated by the Japanese government is an important contribution to the successful implementation of development diplomacy.

Consequently, the implementation of development diplomacy should be treated as a process. Governments in developing countries have only acknowledged its importance with benefits to be realized after the introduction of the new systems, structures and strategies.

This book is not a theoretical treatise; it is based on practical experience. It is purpose driven for those with faith. The hope is that it offers food for thought for those interested in the successful implementation of development diplomacy.

CHAPTER ONE:

DIPLOMACY IN PERSPECTIVE, PAST AND PRESENT

The word diplomacy is a noun meaning statesmanship. It is accurate to describe diplomatic missions as places for conducting matters involving states. The diplomatic missions are in this case representative government offices in foreign countries. It is inaccurate to assume that diplomacy is a new invention by modern states.

The Holy Bible makes reference to diplomacy in the book of 2 Samuel 10:2; King David is reported to have sent a delegation to convey condolences to King Hanun after the death of his father. Similarly, 2 Corinthians 5:20 describe Christian believers as Christ's **ambassadors**. In Ephesians 6:20, the apostle Paul describes himself as an ambassador in chains.

Indeed, the existence of diplomatic missions dates back to historical times. Melissen [1999 p.3] explains that diplomacy had its origin in the ancient kingdom of Elba on the

Mediterranean coast. Breslin [2002 p.61], notes that ancient diplomacy focused on the promotion of economic interests.

The emergence of modern day diplomacy, however, coincided with the time when powers of state were gradually moving from kings to republican states. Olson [1987 p.76] agrees with this view when he explains that it was after the Napoleonic wars that nation states replaced the persona of kings. It was after this development that the practice of diplomacy assumed importance when normalizing discreet processes of states.

With the advent of democracy, the enduring question in developing countries is on the relevance of diplomacy to the lives of citizens. The issue is about value for money. According to Berridge [1995 p.1] , diplomacy is the conduct of international relations by negotiations. The word negotiation implies the existence of two or more parties willing to resolve problems of mutual interest through the spirit of give and take. Other historical views suggest that diplomacy is a complement to war. Contemporary thoughts, however, differ on the type of relationship. The argument is that there is no cause and effect relationship between war and diplomacy. Some believe that the perceived relationship is a matter of strategic choice.

The problem with war is that it is a blunt instrument causing untold misery to women and children. Once people are subjected to war, they adopt two kinds of mindsets. They either resign to exist, or take the aftermath of war as a challenge. The divergence of opinion on coping with war makes the process of confidence building extremely difficult. Therefore, consensus of thought is that diplomacy is a process of making peace. Naturally the characteristic of any process is that it has a definite starting point without an end point. The disadvantage of any process is that it requires time as its main tool. It necessitates patience and money. When countries choose war, it is not because the process of diplomacy has failed. The decision to go to war is made after considering other strategic interests, including military strength and opportunity costs.

Among other things, the anxiety of ordinary citizens regarding diplomacy has been aggravated by the status quo of resident diplomatic missions. Most citizens believe that there should be other means of conducting diplomacy. Indeed, there are many other ways of conducting diplomacy outside the resident diplomatic mission. For instance, diplomacy can be conducted through the exchange of notes, state visits, official visits, attendance at multilateral meetings, sending of special envoys and the use of honorary consuls. Understandably, each method has its own strengths and weaknesses. Therefore, the chosen method has to take into consideration its overall effectiveness. It is obvious that the citizens' concern over the status quo of resident diplomatic missions is due to lack of information. Citizens are unaware of origins of the existing practice of resident diplomatic missions.

According to Melissen [1999 p.4], the first known resident diplomatic representative was recorded at the court of Hammurabi in Mesopotamia, now the Republic of Iraq. The modern form of diplomacy was formalized as a security measure for frequently traveled special envoys. The frequently dispatched special envoys were probably exposed to serious risks.

Apart from the security aspects, there were also cost-benefits that arose from reduced travels and the subsequent informal relations. Those who are familiar with the concept of relationships marketing cannot dispute the value of informal relations when conducting businesses.

The private sector understands the importance of relationships marketing to business development. Almost every business allocates funds for conducting relationships marketing through sports and other social events like lunches and dinners. It is common knowledge that better results in business are achieved from the informality of personal relationships.

The other advantage of resident diplomatic representation is continuity. When the same person is on the ground, it is easier to ensure good understanding as barriers from social distances are eliminated.

With globalization, nearly all civilized countries maintain diplomatic relations of one form or another. In practice two main forms of diplomatic relations exist. One type is known as *bilateral relations*. Bilateral relations characterize the relations between two friendly countries. *Multilateral relations* are when many countries subscribe to the values of the same international institution. In this context, the International Bank for Reconstruction and Development [World Bank] is a multilateral institution because it serves membership of many countries. The United Nations is also another multilateral organization. The annual conference of the World Bank is a multilateral meeting.

Bilateral diplomacy is used when a government deploys a diplomatic note to another government. It is also bilateral diplomacy when a head of state sends a special envoy to another country. Both state and official visits made by heads of state to another state are bilateral visits at highest level. In diplomatic practice, one of the acid tests for assessing the degree of friendship between two states is the visit by the head of state. However, in recent years official visits have become fashionable because they provide flexibility. In spite of the many forms the bilateral relations are conducted, there is no disagreement on the importance of visits by officials among friendly countries. The visits by the heads of state act as political statements to the extent in which friendly states are working together.

In fact such visits give credence to the work of the country's ambassadors on the ground. According to Breslin [2002 p.35], the diplomacy of high level visits was used by ancient Roman governments for the resolution of cross-border skirmishes. This is probably one of the reasons it is common practice for newly elected heads of state to visit neighboring states immediately upon their election. This is to assure the neighbors of good neighborliness. Nyunt [2000 p. 1] also supports this reasoning when he described the protection of territorial integrity as one of the main responsibilities of diplomatic relations.

Pragmatic evidence shows that the practice of diplomacy is not a privilege for a few countries. All civilized countries of the world have to engage in some diplomacy. The only differences are in the purposes for which the diplomatic relations are intended. Every country has diplomatic relations for a purpose. Even those countries which do not have written purpose statements have a reason for maintaining a diplomatic representation.

One form of representation is to gain influence in international politics. The other form is to create confidence in attracting tourism and investors. In the final analysis, a country's posture toward international affairs will be demonstrated through its diplomatic representation.

While history may be replete with wonderful contributions made by diplomacy, the rapidly changing geopolitical situation in today's world has created different perceptions. The general perception by the public in emerging democracies is that diplomacy is synonymous with partisan politics. This misconception is clear from the type of arguments used against the relevance of diplomacy within contemporary systems of government. The arguments inadvertently center on value for money. Obviously, value for money is not easy to show because diplomacy is a long term investment exercise. The efforts of today will pay dividends tomorrow. That is why civilized nations believe that diplomats never retire. They cease to be diplomats only when they die.

`There is no justification for the current poor perception by those who deem diplomacy irrelevant to the functioning of modern governments. On the contrary, democracy as a modern system of government demands strong diplomatic skills. Ideally, diplomacy and democracy should co-exist. The success of one depends on the other. It is the democratic regimes that show us how important diplomacy is in today's world.

There is consensus among many practitioners in diplomacy that public image of the profession suffered during the Cold War. Of course, according to Berridge (1995 p.21), the attempt to draw up international conventions on the practice of diplomacy after the wars of independence was a damage control effort by the international community. After the independence wars, both the emerging states and the former colonial powers had serious reservations as to the best type of working relationships in the new world order. This was why diplomatic conventions were considered important.

The operations of effective diplomacy among the newly independent developing countries became meaningless with the development of the Cold War. Most of the new states associated diplomacy with friendship. Consequently, the developing countries perceived diplomacy as gaining political alignments. In the process, the developing countries became a surrogate force in the Cold War situation for no good reasons. The result was wastage of valuable time and resources. No wonder that until recently most of the developing countries looked at diplomatic relations as a show of friendship.

———————————

Politics is a game of ideologies. No political system can thrive without ideology regardless of where it takes place. Democracy also thrives on ideology by advocating transparency, governance and the rule of law. The Cold War was sustained by career diplomacy and state paternalism. To this end the proponents of the Cold War situation generously supported the operations of makeshift diplomatic schools, research institutes and the mushrooming of state corporations.

Obviously, the state corporations were intended to create employment for the masses at low wages on the basis of state paternalism. Proving that the state corporations, diplomatic training schools and foreign policy research institutes were serving Cold War imperatives, they were the first targets for public sector reforms when competitive multiparty democracy was introduced. The same governments that had promoted the establishment of the institutions became the first to condemn them for being burdensome to taxpayers. This was at least one example in which the Cold War situation misdirected the efforts of the developing states.

Another problem was that during the Cold War; diplomats' behavior and character were important. In fact, one of the qualification traits for a diplomatic position was personal behavior. Those candidates who were soft-spoken and introverted qualified for diplomatic posting irrespective of capabilities.

It is disheartening to listen to stories by former diplomats. Some of them report of having to spend their time on wine tasting sessions. Others talk of lessons on table manners. Berridge [1995. p.5] defends the past practices by saying that ceremonial procedures were an important component of traditional diplomacy, and with good reasons.

Public Accountability

With the consolidation of democratic regimes, ordinary citizens in developing countries have courageously questioned the continued operation of resident diplomatic missions. Politicians from opposition parties have also joined the movement to discredit ruling parties for wasting public funds. The intensity of public discontent against the operations of the diplomatic missions has made the transition to development diplomacy an imperative.

Ordinary citizens believe there is a better way of practicing diplomacy. Some of the citizens have openly indicated their desire to see the immediate privatization of the resident diplomatic missions. Their feeling is that by privatizing the diplomatic missions, direct and indirect taxes would be reduced.

While public service is a national trust for the citizens, it is the responsibility of bureaucrats and elected representatives to balance public opinion against national interests. The bureaucrats and the elected representatives have to make appropriate decisions. When responding to the public outcry, it is necessary to avoid misinterpreting the dissatisfaction as coming from detractors of government programs. Hopeless as it may look, the public is simply asking for value for money and improved service delivery. The citizens have the right to know how their trustees view things. Therefore, they should not be intimidated. James 1:19-20 deplores the tendency of getting angry.

Due to lack of information, the public feeds on rumors from the grapevines. A general perception is that cronyism and nepotism permeate jobs at the diplomatic missions. One can't blame citizens for thinking that way when there is no information. The best solution to eliminate the lack of information, or misinformation, is public education. The government as a public trust belongs to the people. The citizens are therefore entitled to receive and expect respect from their public servants. It is their trust. The public servants, including the elected representatives, have no right to look down upon the citizens.

It is imperative to accept that the liberalization of politics through democracy marked the beginning of a new way of thinking among the citizens. Unlike in the past when policy change was the monopoly of the bureaucrats and elected representatives, it is now the public which will influence policy changes. Nevertheless, the public servants have the responsibility to take the lead in introducing the change. The first change should be the understanding that nothing can work without God's power;

1 Corinthians 1:20 warns that God makes foolish the wisdom of the world.

When understanding the changes, existing culture will also change.

Culture is the lock which permits or delays progressive change in any organization. The unrelenting criticism against the management of diplomatic missions is a good starting point for changing the management culture in the public service including the diplomatic service.

Some of the confusion among the citizens is inevitably a result of the high expectations aroused during the various political campaigns transitioning to democracy. An overwhelming majority of citizens expected seamless political transplants. When changing from dictatorial regimes to competitive multiparty democracies, the expectations were very high. What people did not appreciate was that democracy was not politics, but the process of liberalizing political power to all the citizens. As a process, the subsequent political systems have to evolve from the prevailing cultures, history and social conditions of the respective country.

Nevertheless, it is up to governments to successfully deploy proactive public education strategies for the enlightenment of their citizens. There is no short cut to the dissemination of public information. It is a matter of moving together with the people on the daunting road to peaceful coexistence and national development. Public education is needed for everyone to understand what purposes development diplomacy is expected to achieve. Obviously development democracy does not mean merely receiving handouts in the form of Official Development Assistance (ODA) from donors.

The scriptures discourage the attitude of laziness in 1 Thessalonians 4: 11-12 when Paul is advising believers to earn respect for themselves by being self-reliant. Each country must create its own identity in order to attract investors. The process is not unlike the person wanting to marry. Such a person has to dress well to be viewed as attractive for marriage.

Therefore, it is necessary to appreciate the importance of country specific identities. Every country has natural gifts from God to be used responsibly. Some countries have rain forests, while others have beautiful mountains. Some have minerals, and others have highly skilled people. All these gifts are given to the people of the respective country by God. It is a matter of choosing which gift to use as the country's identity.

In a new world order in which democracy is the common denominator, obviously it is necessary for some government functions to change. The politics of the past required different policy postures aimed at achieving ideological alignments. Consequently, some departments of government assumed more importance than others, becoming stepping stones to more senior positions in the country. In democratic environments, the role of some government departments also need to change to meet the new development challenges.

The Systems Management View

The foregoing perspective helps to demonstrate that it is incorrect for citizens of any country to view development diplomacy as a discreet function that must be performed in foreign countries. There is nothing that functions in exclusion. Life is simply an interconnection of many things.

For instance, human beings depend on oxygen manufactured by trees during photosynthesis. One of the important raw materials required for the process of manufacturing oxygen is carbon dioxide, which is generated by flue gases from industries and exhaust fumes from motor vehicles. While carbon dioxide is bad for humans, it is good for the trees. In other words, rather than looking at the effectiveness of diplomatic missions solely in the unitary sense, the correct approach should be to look at the systems management view of the whole government.

The scriptures emphasize the importance of this view in Romans 12:4 when the apostle Paul talks about the concept of one body with many members, performing different functions.

Mother Nature offers many examples to demonstrate how things co-exist in life; the human body is one such good example. The human body comprises many organs. In spite of that fact, no person is known by the name of any single body organ. In this sense, the human body can be described as the major system, while the individual body organs are sub-systems to the major system. A healthy body means that all the body organs, which in this case are the sub-systems, are working together in harmony. When one organ or sub-system is not functioning at the same pace with the other organs, the body is said to be sick and out of harmony, and that person eventually admits to being sick, sometimes to the point of hospitalization.

Likewise, the same applies to the means in which diplomatic missions operate. Functionally they are only parts of the major system, which is their government. Diplomatic missions do not operate independently from their government. Traditionally, governments use classical management approaches aimed at adhering to the ethics of consistency, equality and fairness. The ethics are sustained by the issuance of rules and procedures on a regular basis. Oftentimes, the public sector is notorious for an overdependence on rules and procedures.

Unfortunately, some rules and regulations lose the purpose for which they were originally intended immediately upon their circulation. In most cases, they are incoherent, subjective and irrelevant to the changing situations. Management efficiency requires the application of proactive decisions and quick adaptation to the rapidly changing situations on the ground. This is one of the traits that differentiate the private and public sectors. The private sector usually makes decisions to suit a specific situation. This is why private sector managers are often successful – especially when compared to their public sector counterparts.

Even government departments responsible for national educational programs recognize the importance of revising their curriculums from time to time in order to adapt to scientific and technological advances. Imagine what would have happened if some developing countries resisted the introduction of the computer for the slide ruler? The slide ruler had served its own time – it has now been surpassed by the computer. This demonstrates why managing by rules and procedure alone is considered the first obstacle to management efficiency. Unless this practice is changed, the implementation of development diplomacy will be a difficult task.

Understandably, governments cannot operate in exactly the same way private sector organizations do. The two institutions have different operating objectives. It is well known that the private sector satisfies exclusive demands through the markets, while the public sector addresses the needs of its' citizens. The servicing of needs has no profit objectives. What is required when servicing citizens' needs is a smart integration of management systems. Development diplomacy is a relationship marketing function. Those who have studied marketing would agree that marketing succeeds on the creation of product identity. Without creating a country's identity, any efforts to promote development diplomacy will be hamstrung.

Development diplomacy should indeed be perceived as a marketing function geared toward long term results. The work being done today at diplomatic missions will yield results in years to come. However, there is tangible need for diplomatic representatives to gain an appreciation and respect for effective planning and decision making skills. The diplomatic representatives have to understand the concepts of balancing resource requirements against available resources. It is simply the ability of achieving or producing more with fewer resources.

Diplomatic representatives are also expected to successfully balance responsibility and accountability for actions under their control. An effective control requires correspondence between accountability and responsibility. Unlike war, diplomacy demands time and substantial amounts of money. Efforts to label diplomacy as a public good have added salt to injury. In modern classification, diplomacy is neither a social nor economic function. Many people view diplomacy as a state apparatus. But how is the function expected to work effectively when it is hamstrung by identity problems within government itself?

In spite of lauding development diplomacy as the solution to poverty, public perception is that of a state apparatus. This is the origin of the confusion. The fact is that diplomacy is a cross cutting function. It has assumed an economic status by embracing the concept of development diplomacy. Therefore it is wrong to perceive diplomacy solely as a state function. Diplomacy and democracy must co-exist. It is incumbent upon governments to provide continuous public education on what diplomacy is and is not.

REFERENCES:

Berridge.G.R.[1995] – Diplomacy–Theory and Practice,
1st Edition London,
Prentice Hall

Melissen.J [1999] – Innovation in Diplomatic Practice, 1st
Edition, London, Macmillan Press LTD.

Breslin. T.A-[2002] – Beyond Pain- The Role of Pleasure and
Culture in Making of Foreign Affairs, 1st
Edition
United of America, Praeger Publishers,

Olson. W [1987] – The Theory and Practice
of International Relations
7th Edn, USA
Prentice Hall-Inc

Nyunt.Gen [2000] – Heads of Mission Conference
Myanmar News 3/2000.
Bible: New International Version (NIV)

CHAPTER TWO:

MANAGEMENT CULTURE

All believers in the teachings of Jesus Christ are members of one body. The scriptures confirm this in 1 Corinthians 12:13 by saying that believers are baptized by one spirit into one body. As members of one body they share the word of God in the Holy Bible. One of the many shared values by Christians is forgiveness. Another is perseverance. It is these shared values among others which form and distinguish Christian culture. When believers in Jesus Christ meet together, they behave differently from unbelievers in the way they communicate.

Shared values are not exclusive to Christian believers, however. All groups of people, including commercial organizations, have shared values. It is these shared values which distinguish groups and organizations from one another.

Diplomatic missions are no exception. Over the years, they have developed their own culture of management which makes them operate the way they do. In other words, it is the culture that manifests current management practices at the diplomatic missions. When citizens complain about poor management at diplomatic missions, they are actually questioning the culture. Consequently, when implementing development diplomacy, it is incumbent for governments to consider changing the existing cultures. The necessary changes cannot be achieved in a haphazard manner, however; there is a need for a holistic approach towards the changes.

There is consensus that all business organizations are a reflection of the behavior and attitudes of their employees. The same applies to religious institutions. In spite of sharing similar doctrines, the religious institutions do not have the same public images. It is the different behavior and attitude by members to the organizations that create the public perceptions. It is, therefore, wrong for citizens to associate the existing culture at diplomatic missions with those institutions. If institutions were creating culture, there would have been no differences between them. All institutions would have the same reputation. But that does not happen in practice. Instead, it is not unusual to see distinctive differences between banks, schools, churches and even diplomatic missions. For instance, some churches have more members than others, and some schools have better students than others. In either case, it is not about the business or organization, but the people and leadership involved.

The previous chapter has shown that diplomatic missions operate as delivery pipes for government's rules and procedures. The justification for the top down management approach is usually given as a need to maintain consistency. The consequence of management by rules and procedures is inevitably poor management. This management of rules and procedures muzzles creativity and the capacity of decision making. Ultimately, the employees, including the ambassador, become reactive and passive recipients of policy. It is therefore a waste of public resources to have senior diplomats at the level of ambassadors not making decisions.

Maintaining figureheads in foreign countries removes the challenges from the job. Honestly, control of routine activities does not require the involvement of senior management. The best approach is to match public image with responsibility and accountability.

The practice demonstrates the effectiveness of the power of status symbols, which was one of the management tools used by the colonizing powers. Ordinarily, all diplomatic missions are headed by ambassadors, and if within the British Commonwealth, by high commissioners. Depending on the size of the diplomatic mission, there could be a deputy ambassador or deputy high commissioner. Additionally, there could also be a minister/counsellor at the same diplomatic mission. Considering that the ambassadors/high commissioners are not expected to make decisions, it is not wrong when ordinary citizens complain about poor resource management at the diplomatic missions. As discussed elsewhere, one of the principles of management by exception demands that the degree of control has to be relative to the activity being controlled. If the staff at diplomatic missions cannot make decisions, even when they have the competence to do so, it is evidence of poor human resource management. Therefore, instead of perceiving the public reaction negatively, it is advisable to listen and take the necessary corrective action.

There is compelling evidence that some diplomatic missions are over- staffed. This is due to the traditional practice of posting staff to diplomatic missions without conducting human resource requirement planning. Overstaffing is a direct indicator of poor resource management, and these mistakes occur due to the absence of decision making powers at the diplomatic missions. For instance, ambassadors generally learn about the arrival of new staff after the decision has already been made. And when attempts are made to seek clarifications on such postings, the answer is often assigned to directives in abstract terms.

Obviously the first casualty in these instances is morale. By sidelining the ambassador from the decision making process, the initiative of control is also taken away. Consequently, new staffers arriving at the diplomatic mission have no job descriptions. And when the new staffs have no job description, there is no way job performance can be monitored. Performance monitoring requires standards, because monitoring means weighing actual results against standards.

Cross Cultural Influences

One of the responsibilities of diplomatic missions is promoting cross cultural exchange. Diplomatic missions are not only supposed to focus on trade, tourism, and investment opportunities, but also the promotion of cultural exchange. This is why some governments strategically offer employment to citizens of the country in which the diplomatic mission is located. Usually, there is a mix between transferred staff and locally recruited staff.

Some diplomatic missions employ cooks from the homeland of the ambassador for the purpose of preparing traditional cuisine to guests at the official residence. It is easy to discourage such a practice on the premise of the expense, but to the contrary, it is part of the marketing strategy in promoting national culture. In this way, the official residence becomes the show window for different food cultures from the sending state.

In view of the desire to promote development diplomacy by developing countries, the policy has never been as relevant as it is now. The practice is not new to developed countries. The developed countries have always maintained the services of cooks from their homelands at diplomatic missions in an effort to project the cultural identities of their nations. Unlike in the past when the primary business of diplomatic missions was political diplomacy, development diplomacy is expensive as such costs cannot be avoided.

Apart from the food diplomacy and consistent with the desire to expand people-to-people friendship, almost all diplomatic missions worldwide employ local citizens from their country of assignment. The management of the diplomatic mission is undertaken by the transferred staff from the capitals of the sending states. The transferred staff work on term assignments and are commonly known as the diplomatic staff. They constitute the management teams at the diplomatic mission. "Management" in this case is used loosely pertaining to the diplomatic staff. Indeed, the whole concept of management is a fallacy when applied to the diplomatic missions because no one can become a manager without relevant training. And because management requires experience, it is no wonder that some diplomatic missions experience poor resource management problems.

The recruitment of local staff is on local employment terms, based on the labor practices in the country of assignment. The staff combination has hidden benefits to cost reduction as the local staff compliment is less expensive to maintain.

When offering employment to the local staff, it is important to ensure full compliance to the labor laws of the country. However, the decision on which jobs to extend to locally recruited staff is a difficult policy issue. The legacy of treating ambassadors as passive recipients of rules and procedures under the guise of maintaining consistency continues to hinder progress in this area. Considering that promotion of trade, tourism and investments is not sensitive, it is advisable for some of these jobs to be offered to local staff. Some diplomatic missions from developing countries which have tried offering such jobs to the locally recruited staff claim to have realized benefits from the risk.

Obviously it should be more effective to deploy the services of locally recruited staff on trade and tourism promotion than transferred staff. The local staffs know the culture and geography of the capitals, and therefore waste little time to conclude business deals. The precondition for success in the innovation is the availability of brochures and incentive packages to reinforce good performance. Useful brochures should be translated in the popular native language of the country of assignment.

It is a well-known business tactic that successful deals require confidence building measures, in which case the use of locally recruited staff is a smart choice. The only problem is the need for appropriate incentives proportionate to achieved results. Therefore, the use of locally recruited staff in the promotion of trade, tourism and investments should depend on how much decision-making powers are assigned to the ambassador or high commissioner, because there is need for performance measurement systems and payment of performance related monetary incentives. Rewards must be paid on time for effectiveness. In Matthew 25: 14-30 the

Lord Jesus Christ explains the importance of rewards and punishment through the parable of the three servants and their talents.

In recent years, for strategic reasons some governments have included the appointment of non-bureaucrats from outside public service. Usually the objective is to match jobs with skills for optimum benefits, the logic being to ensure that diplomatic missions are managed by people with different skills and backgrounds. This is a good strategy for the promotion of development diplomacy. With every country pursuing development diplomacy, investors find it difficult to choose suitable destinations for their investment capital. A professional presentation at the diplomatic mission makes the difference when attracting potential investors. First impression is important because investors have no time to waste on unproductive meetings with uninformed people.

Just like any new idea, the emergence of non-bureaucrats into a closed profession has not been without problems. Bureaucrats responsible for funding the day-to-day operations of diplomatic missions have increased the probability that the outsiders' efforts would fail. The aim of these bureaucrats is to prove that not everyone is made for diplomatic work. This is why there are invocations for career diplomacy in order to restrict the influx of non-bureaucrats into the profession. Inevitably the greed is being advanced without taking cognizance of the implications of the bill of rights incorporated in most democratic constitutions. Specifically, the bill of rights makes it unlawful to discriminate in the work place.

It is a contravention of basic human rights for citizens to be discriminated from national employment opportunities; it is also illegal under democratic constitutions for such practices to continue at the work place. It is also morally wrong for one group of employees to practice protectionism on baseless grounds.

It has already been pointed out in the previous chapter that diplomatic careerism was one of the tools used to sustain the Cold War. It is advisable for Governments in developing countries not be overwhelmed by buzz-words. Buzzwords come and go. Nature provides good lessons on the importance of cross breeding to the genetics of reproduction. Efficiency cannot be improved without systems. That would be an oversimplification of the serious problems negatively affecting performance in the first place.

There is a pressing need to incorporate the systems management approach to diplomacy in order to eradicate policy disconnects. A farm tractor cannot till the land at the farm simply because it is parked there. For the tractor to work it needs oil, diesel fuel, brake fluid and good tires with traction – otherwise it will sit idle.

The other prerequisite for improving performance at diplomatic missions is a reward system offering incentives for hard work. Good performance is a factor of judgment, commitment and flexibility. The imposition of inflexible rules and procedures does not provide the opportunity to make good decisions.

Culture of Postings and Recalls

"Posting" describes the process of moving a transferred staff to take a diplomatic post. "Similarly recall" means the process of returning home by the transferred staff after serving in the diplomatic service. One of the most difficult issues is management of these staff movements. While both words have straightforward meanings, the process of implementing them is not that simple. Indeed, staff postings and recalls are very complicated to manage because both activities have emotional effects. Understandably, both actions have psychological implications for those involved.

Appointees would like to leave immediately to assume their duties upon being advised of their appointment. Any delay in receiving posting instructions is considered sabotage. Unfortunately, it is not always possible for the appointed officer to leave immediately because of funding problems. Frequently, the logistics officer at the line ministry is blamed for such delays, and any attempt to explain the real cause of the delay is received with mixed feelings.

One such problem the logistics officer faces is the availability of funding. Funding is controlled by a different government department – one with its own priorities. It observes its own decision rules, and public revenue collection is seasonal; therefore, its collection varies. Consequently, posting instruction coinciding within such a period when public revenue is low causes delays.

Like anything else, it is unreasonable to expect expenditure on the posting of diplomatic staff to take priority over purchasing of medicines for local citizens in the public hospital. This is just one dilemma the logistics officer is confronted with when implementing a posting instruction. The delay is not meant personally, but it is often taken that way by those waiting to leave on postings. In this case, the logistics officer's position is suitable for individuals with high empathy levels. Individuals with weak personalities wouldn't last on the job before suffering from heart failure, anxiety attacks or ulcers.

However, this does not exonerate envious bureaucrats deliberately delaying the process. There are sometimes individuals who do not like to see or hear about the success of others. This is a prevailing attitude in traditional communities. Such communities are driven by the motive of power of the group as opposed to that of the individual. In other words everyone must be equal. When one member of the group succeeds, the rest of the group reacts negatively, and the group becomes infected by resentment. Mbigi/Maree [1995. p 7] agrees that disadvantaged groups anywhere in the world survive on collective solidarity due to the poverty of their material circumstances. Jealousy arises from the realization that diplomatic posting offers unparalleled opportunities to those back at home. Children of diplomats receive better education in foreign countries and better exposure upon their return. Another factor causing jealousy is the knowledge that every diplomat brings back a good car following the Foreign Service posting.

The other obstacle to diplomatic postings is the prevalence of power politics within government. When an individual is appointed to assume a Foreign Service post, divergent political forces are immediately energized; many contradictory comments come to the fore. Some of the political forces are so negative that the appointment is stifled. There are many people who have been appointed but failed to assume the posts due to unexplained reasons. Needless to say the situations create considerable pain to those affected. The tendency of judging others is discouraged in Matthew 7: 1-2 by the warning that such judgment is for God.

Usually the appointment of new diplomats is for the purpose of replacing those who have been recalled to home service. As previously noted, the implementation of staff recalls is also a complex issue. It is natural for human beings to resist change. Generally diplomats, especially their families, resist recall instructions. While human nature would be cited as the main reason, one would think that there is a need to review the way in which recall instructions are issued. Sometimes, it is the way the instructions are conveyed that causes the problems.

The behavior of some bureaucrats may be one reason recall instructions are challenged. In the first place, a recall is an emotional subject. Depending on the way it is communicated, it can be welcome or sad news; therefore, it has to be conveyed humanely. Ideally the starting point should be consultation. A face to face meeting back home would provide the opportunity to share experiences and discuss the decision for the recall. Such a consultation would avail the opportunity of conducting an appraisal of any achievements made. The personal interaction is preferable because the scriptures in Matthew 12:34 says that the mouth speaks what is full in the heart.

Obviously, the face to face interaction might help to pacify and strengthen relationships. Money should not be used as the excuse for failing to undertake these consultations. The principle should always be "love one another." The scriptures in 1 John 3:11-15 says that anyone who does not love remains in death. It is important to remember that people have personal feelings, and unless these feelings are respected, the outcome could be unnecessary disagreements.

It is always good courtesy to recognize achievement made by others. Some countries have the practice of conferring national awards for good performance in the diplomatic service. When discussing a recall, bureaucrats should change their attitudes and put themselves in the diplomat's position. In other words, "do unto others as you would have them do unto you." The tendency of using recalls to humiliate those affected should be discouraged.

Budgetary constraints should not be used as the excuse for failure to promote good human relations with the diplomatic staff during recalls. No government has extra money. Understandably, the money situation is even worse in the developing countries which rely on balance of payment support from cooperating partners. It is simply a balancing act driven by shifting priorities. All that is needed is planning for the expenditure. Money is never available in unlimited supply. Even in the private sector where the motive is profit optimization, there is no industry that does not experience money problems.

Changing the status quo is necessary if implementing diplomacy for development is to succeed. How does one attract foreign direct investment when the marketplace is highly competitive? It is only by facing the competition. How does one promote trade when the process of decision making takes months? Potential investors tend to lose interest in dealing with officials who lack authority. The business community believes that it takes money to make money. Even the person who wins a lottery spends money first to buy the entry ticket; it is indeed a chicken and egg situation.

Similarly, business people follow market efficiencies and not just names of countries. Development diplomacy will not produce any positive results if the diplomatic missions continue to operate as delivery pipes of rules and procedures.

A quick investigation on the expenditure patterns of public revenue show that out of all the expenses at diplomatic missions, substantial amount of money is spent on recalls. Closer looks at the recall expenses also show a positive correlation between the level of expenditure and the service periods. The shorter the service periods the higher the amount of money spent on recalls. Similarly, the shorter the service periods the more frequent the postings. In that regard, the costs associated with postings and recalls reflect the weakness of public policy on movement of staff and their families.

Cost savings could be realized when some of the current policies on service periods are reviewed. Costs on transfer of staff between diplomatic missions can also be high when administered incorrectly. The transfers between diplomatic missions unless centrally controlled can also create higher cost burdens to public expenditure. Such transfers should be entertained when the objective is to improve efficiency at the other diplomatic mission based on competence and capabilities. Ideally, transfer between diplomatic missions is not a cost reduction strategy but rather an efficiency improvement measure.

It is clear that the current public debate against management at diplomatic missions is not mere speculation. It is correct in a way. However, it is necessary for the citizens to know that living allowances paid to the diplomatic staff in the foreign countries are not salaries. The allowances are intended to help the diplomatic staff live in the foreign capitals. Unlike local salaries the allowances are not adjusted to cover inflationary fluctuations; some countries take many years to review the allowances. In extreme cases, some of the living allowances are adjusted downwards in times of economic difficulties.

Substantial amount of public revenue is spent on air tickets and sea freight which change all the time. Whenever posting and recall instructions are issued, it is the time more money from taxes is spent. Sometimes the difficulty is the means in which public expenses are treated by the administration at headquarters. Generally the costs are shrouded into general administrative expenses making direct accountability difficult. Ideally, posting and recall costs should be charged to the respective cost centre instead of being treated as general administration expenditure at headquarters.

Apparently, there is no standard service period in the international community. The length of the service period is a policy decision made by each government. However, most countries use an average of four years. Some governments have a flexible policy over recalls, which are among other things influenced by the prevailing culture in the country of accreditation and performance of the diplomat.

Depending on the development stage of the sending country and when all things are equal, it is advisable for ambassadors to serve at strategic diplomatic missions longer. The longer they serve at the strategic mission, the greater the chance for them to assume the status of diplomatic corps dean.

While the diplomatic corps deanship is an honorific status, it helps to uplift the identity and image of the sending state. This is a relationships marketing strategy which smaller states could use to make themselves better known in strategic locations. In the end, the benefit would go to the sending state and not the individual diplomat.

Development diplomacy is not the same passive game as was political diplomacy. Development diplomacy involves the promotion of business interests; therefore, it requires the use of winning strategies. Gradually, governments must come to terms with strategic management in order to play the game better.

When discussing public expenditure culture, it is also imperative to consider the effects of foreign trips by bureaucrats. External travel irrespective of who undertakes it, is expensive. Unless controlled, it may have the same effect on public budget as postings and recalls. There is always justification for undertaking external travels. However, with the presence of diplomatic missions, it should be possible to appoint the resident ambassador as an envoy at international meetings. The traditional practice of associating attendance at international meetings with the travel of officials from the sending governments should therefore be reviewed. In recent years, it is unfortunate that some of the international conferences have inevitably become nothing more than promotion of tourism.

In some developed countries, it is not unusual to maximize benefits from foreign exchange movements during such international meetings. Therefore, the more conferences hosted, the higher the tourism income for the hosting country.

There is a need to review current policies on external travel in the holistic sense. It does not matter who is involved in the external travel. External travel costs money which could be used to buy medicines for public hospitals and exercise books for elementary schools. Therefore, there is a need to conduct a cost benefit analysis before undertaking such travel. The correct approach should not be to view public expenditure control from the standpoint of others. Effective public expenditure management cannot be achieved when the approach is not holistic. Effective expenditure control requires exemplary leadership. Leadership should not be sought in order to control others. Good leadership must begin with the individual before extending it to others. The scriptures in Psalm 139 23-24 say that good leaders must have a heart that has been searched by God. This is a shared value among

Christians that centers on the love for others. Expenditure control has to be systematic and inclusive.

Another point to ponder is that public services are ongoing institutions where job training is its hallmark. Therefore, it is only when governments introduce the systems management view that genuine cost reduction will be realized.

REFERENCES:

Mbigi.L/Maree.J [1995] – Ubuntu- The Spirit of African Transformation Management, 2nd Edn, Sigma Press, Pretoria South Africa.

CHAPTER THREE:

PLANNING AND DECISION MAKING

Planning simply means organizing resources for effective utilization in the future. Believers in Jesus Christ plan their life daily by placing their hope in the living God. It is a continuous process. Christian believers do not rest idly planning for their lives. They read the Holy Bible daily and serve others. This is consistent with the fact that Christianity is not only a matter of gaining knowledge of the Bible but also actions. James 1:22-23 says that faith without deeds is useless.

When one places one's hope in Jesus Christ, God automatically becomes the controller. For believers, the notion of control involves being monitored by God. The standards which Christians use are written in the Holy Bible. When one has no faith in Jesus Christ, one cannot claim to have one's life under the control of God. Unbelievers do not have their life under the control of the living God, but rather yield that control to other things. Proverbs 29:18a says that where there is no revelation, the people cast off restraint.

At the work place, planning is also key to success. Without planning, there can be no monitoring and control. The plan becomes a standard against which actual results are measured. In this respect, the standard at the work place could be a physical product, drawing or color. When there is a standard, decision making is simplified. Bennett [1994 p 63] argues that planning and decision making cannot be separated. He believes that planning means deciding now what is to be done in the future. He also acknowledges that the process of planning is both troublesome and expensive.

It is troublesome because of the need to look into the future, but of course no one can predict the future with absolute certainty. It is expensive because planning takes time. Management planning involves the use of large volumes of paper, including field opinion. The advantages of management planning far exceed the disadvantages. The first advantage is that it helps to eliminate wastage of time. The second advantage is that it reveals the unnecessary duplication of resources. Management planning also helps highlight potential bottlenecks. Finally, planning provides management with the necessary information for the evaluation of performance through the establishment of standards and targets. In this sense, planning may be described as the fuel for productivity improvement. High levels of productivity cannot be achieved without prior planning.

Therefore, there cannot be resource productivity improvement at diplomatic missions without the planning process. It must be accepted from the outset that there are preconditions for effective planning. For instance, effective planning requires the availability of purpose statements. The statement of purpose helps to describe the reason for the establishment of an organization. David [1998. p. 83] adds by suggesting that a statement of purpose defines the business in which the organization is involved.

This is correct owing to the fact that all successful organizations are established with a purpose to achieve. It is incorrect to assume that the purpose for the operation of diplomatic missions will be implied from the foreign policy statements which most governments issue periodically. It is also incorrect for governments to assume that international diplomatic conventions provide the primary purposes for the operation of diplomatic missions. The fact that every country has unique social, economic and political challenges makes it imperative for each diplomatic mission to have a specific purpose statement. Quinn [1998. p. 6] agrees that a well formulated purpose statement helps to marshal and allocate an organization's resources into an unique and variable posture relative to environmental changes.

The statement of purpose commonly known in private sector organizations as the mission statement helps those organizations when preparing operational objectives and performance targets. David [1998. p. 80] supports this view when he notes that a clear statement of purpose is essential for the establishment of business objectives and the formulation of performance targets. In other words, David believes that the statement of purpose describes the business of the organization. [1998. ibid] Unless an organization's purpose is known, the outcome will be confusion. Consequently, it should not be unusual to find diplomatic missions from the same government possessing different statements of purpose. The purpose statements have to be crafted in such a way that they facilitate the realization of maximum benefits from the country of accreditation.

Thisunderlinestheimportanceofintroducingmanagement planning and decision making at the diplomatic missions. Obviously it puts into question the long standing tradition of expecting diplomatic missions to operate from foreign policy documents. With due respect, the foreign policy documents contain general statements in the form of policy frameworks. Therefore, it is unrealistic to expect any positive contributions from the diplomatic missions when they operate without specific purpose statements. Ideally, each diplomatic mission should produce its own statement of purpose, including objectives and targets for measurement of achievements.

The purpose statements, objectives and targets should be mutually agreed by all those whose performance is to be monitored upon at the beginning of each year. There should be no illusions of perceiving the creation of purpose statements and targets as an end. Implementations of these strategic issues demand the use of resources and time. This is what Ranson/Stewart [1994. p. 16] warn against when they say that operational requirements and the routines of administration can sometimes become dominant in a way that presents barriers to organization's performance. What they mean is that there should be relationship between policy and strategy. In this case, the writing of purpose statements is one thing; their implementation is another.

Obviously, diplomatic missions operating without statements of purpose lose their focus; useful time is wasted on less productive activities. The lack of purpose statements is probably the single greatest cause of poor resource management at the diplomatic missions. It is unbelievable that presently, most diplomatic missions continue to operate as mere delivery pipes of rules and procedures. Ranson/ Stewart [1994. p. 19] argue that the distinguishing feature of a public office is the political character of its products. The general misconception is that running a diplomatic mission is the same as running any other public office. Under this premise, bureaucrats at headquarters would like to exercise remote control over the day-to-day management of diplomatic missions through the issuance of incoherent rules and procedures.

Rules and procedures achieve nothing more than incapacitating initiative and creativity among the staffs at diplomatic missions. Bennett [1994. p. 64] thinks that the bureaucratic top down approach is a compensatory strategy for skill deficiencies. If the skill deficiency is at fault, the best alternative would be to implement the practice of management by exception. Only those staffers exhibiting skill deficiency should be targeted for the bureaucratic top down management approach.

It serves no purpose for bureaucrats to separate accountability from responsibility at the spot where the action takes place. Johnson/Scholes [1997. p. 89] agree that bureaucrats tend to simplify complexities associated within the operational environment by relying too much on historical or outdated information.

The foregoing information provides empirical evidence that the best means of improving resource management at diplomatic missions is by introducing the practice of preparing purpose statements, objectives and targets. Fortunately, there is neither standard content nor a standard length for purpose statements. The length and content would depend on the strategic interests being pursued. Most importantly, the statement of purpose should highlight the reason for the establishment of the diplomatic mission at the existing or proposed location.

In the final analysis, the statement of purpose becomes an integral part of the strategic posture of the government being represented in the country of accreditation. It provides the means for implementing and evaluating strategic activities – without personalizing issues. In the absence of statements of purpose, Johnson/Scholes [1999. p. 244] agree that regulations and procedures become the purpose. It is no wonder that ordinary citizens question the operations of the diplomatic missions. If all diplomatic missions had statements of purpose, together with operational objectives and performance targets, there would be no problems providing explanations.

It is encouraging to note that some governments have incorporated the strategic management concept of purpose statements as a means of reforming public sector practices. Consequently, the purpose statements are being introduced at many diplomatic missions. Gratefully, purpose statements have the effect of becoming value statements for employees in an organization. When used properly, the purpose statements act as the social glue binding all employees together.

At no time should the introduction of purpose statements be associated with hidden objectives. The scriptures warn against the practice of lying. Romans 1:25 explains that some people exchange the truth for lies. Therefore, it is advisable for all public employees to get involved in the preparation of these purpose statements.

If the aim of introducing purpose statements at diplomatic missions is motivated by the attitude of punishing certain individuals, Johnson/Scholes [1999. p. 243] believe that their production will be merely lip-service. Statements of purpose should be prepared by all government departments without exception. Only after the government has issued its core purpose statement should individual departments be expected to prepare theirs. The departmental purpose statements should dovetail into the government's core statement to ensure synergy and integration.

It is the purpose statement which distinguishes one organization from the other. The purpose statement projects the values the organization places on its operations and clients. It is only through the purpose statement that it is possible to establish operational objectives and performance targets to leverage on country specific comparative advantages. It is well known that the drafting of a statement of purpose does not in itself result in improved resource management; however, it is a starting point.

After the purpose statement is developed, there is need to create operating objectives and performance targets. Without the operational objectives, it is impossible to achieve anything. Similarly, having objectives alone without performance targets for monitoring achievements is also not enough. Monitoring performance is possible only when there are targets. It is illogical to expect resource management improvements in the absence of operating objectives and targets.

Decision Making

Decision making requires sound judgment. Good judgment is based on facts. Facts can be obtained from books or experience. However, there are some people who are afraid of making decisions. When such people muster the courage to make decisions, the result is a cluster of inconsistencies. On the other hand, there are those who want to make decisions even when they do not have facts. In the extreme, there are those who want to be involved in every decision making process, even when the issue is beyond their knowledge.

The scriptures are unequivocal when it comes to decision making. Acts 6:3 recommends that decision makers should be people full of the Spirit and wisdom. This means that good decisions can only be made by competent people having the facts. Decisions have to be made while remembering that some of the outcome may be unexpected. The ethical consideration for good decision making is observance of the principles of accountability, objectivity and common good. When these values are observed, there should be no reason to interfere in the decision making process. It is public accountability that matters most when making decision. The belief should always be that God is always present when decisions are made. Romans 13:14 advises decision makers to clothe themselves with the Lord Jesus Christ in order to avoid sinful influences.

As discussed previously, governments are notorious for issuing rules and procedures. The aim of rules and procedures should be to act as guidelines, and also to ensure that decisions are consistent and mutually reinforcing to the overriding objectives of the whole government. Mullins (1996 p. 300) argues that the quality of decisions among other things

42

depend upon the quality of an organization's objectives. This underlines the importance of participatory management when preparing purpose statements and operating objectives. Purpose statements should be prepared by all the employees who will use them. At no time should purpose statements be used as tools for punishments. Operating objectives should be realistic, transparent and achievable.

It is important to appreciate that no one can make decisions without information. The first piece of information presenting the facts is the purpose statement. This, together with the operating objectives, provides the challenges and vision of the organization. The objectives must be clear and specific in order to eliminate ambiguity. Good objectives must assist the decision making process. Clear objectives have the added advantage of helping to improve internal communication.

Decision making is an ongoing process punctuated by evaluations. Any deviation from expected results requires corrective action to ensure that the results are in line with the original objectives. However, Mullins (1996 p. 301) warns that the objectives should not hinder the recognition of new opportunities, potential dangers, staff initiatives and innovation. There must always be flexibility.

It is incorrect to assume that all decisions will be good or right. Some decisions will be bad. However, the fear of making a wrong or bad decision should never be justification for refusing to make decisions. So long as the decisions do not harm public image and are consistent with the teachings in the Bible, there should be no reason to fear being decisive. The positive side of making bad decisions should be learning from the mistake.

Logically, one could safely conclude that the poor management problems at most diplomatic missions are a result of the absence of decision making. Diplomatic missions are by nature strategic institutions. Working situations rapidly change, and correct decisions have to be made on the spot without delay. The concept of strategy involves the maintenance of balance between a limited resource and its environment. Therefore, diplomatic missions in foreign countries have to seize on market opportunities by making timely decisions. In the face of increased competition, the ability to benefit from market opportunities requires speedy decision making. Delays in responding to strategic situations in a timely manner may result in the loss of investment opportunities.

It follows naturally that governments should desist from the temptation of exercising unnecessary bureaucratic control over their diplomatic missions. Instead, they should work on appointing experienced, professionally trained staff. The most important requirement is that they are capable of making good decisions; bearing in mind that good decisions demand the correspondence of responsibility and accountability. The two must co-exist at the point of action. There is no way diplomatic missions can assume responsibility over resource management efficiency when decisions are made elsewhere. Centralizing responsibility cannot be possible without corresponding accountability; the two are mutually exclusive. In the end, diplomatic missions should not be blamed for failure to perform when the decision making process is based elsewhere.

Developing countries have become obsessed by the desire to promote development diplomacy. Most of them, however, are succumbing to the utopian views of careerism and elitism. Whether or not they are aware, development diplomacy cannot succeed when diplomatic missions have no decision making powers. It does not matter who is appointed for the jobs. What matters is speed in which decisions are made. Development diplomacy is an interface between the public and private sectors. Apart from decision making, diplomatic missions should also appreciate the importance of time. Of paramount importance is the ability to match capabilities to ever-changing situations on the ground. There is a need for the diplomatic staff to have the ability of developing networks and coalitions of partners.

Sometimes there is a misconception of equating the delegation of decision making to independence. Control can still be retained at headquarters through interactive reporting systems. All that is required is effective monitoring through regular inspections. In this case, policy in the context of operational guidelines cannot be over emphasized. After the devolution of decision making powers, it is imperative to strengthen reporting and monitoring systems. This is the manner in which global companies survive.

Targets

Targets are standards against which performance can be measured. The use of targets helps to eliminate subjectivity. In the absence of targets, decision making is left to individual whims. The view is advocated by apostle Paul in Philippians 3: 14 when he says that targets help focusing on award wining tasks. By introducing targets at diplomatic missions, it will be possible to measure and control performance. The supervisors at headquarters will no longer pay attention to friends. Obviously, promotions to senior grades would be made on merit. However, the general consensus is that targets only work when there are products to measure.

But diplomatic missions aren't businesses – there are no products or units to measure. How would diplomatic work be measured? This is the usual excuse from scoring the effectiveness of diplomatic missions. Bennett [1994. p. 104] supports these views by saying that it is not easy to measure the performance of advisors in numerical terms. He goes further to warn against the danger of attempting to quantify activities that are unquantifiable for the sake of measurements.

It is correct that target setting demands objectivity. Never should it be used as a clandestine tool for punishing employees. Employees should perceive target setting as the means for their career advancements. This means that targets should be agreed upon by all the staff at the diplomatic mission. All the staffs should acknowledge fairness in those values to be used as targets. The advantage of involving the staff when setting targets is the ultimate motivational effect. The targets themselves become shared values for the employees; subsequently, this enhances human relations. Therefore, it is wrong to introduce targets without proper explanations and performance reinforcing mechanisms.

Achieving targets deserves positive recognition through a system of rewards. Consequently, those diplomatic missions doing better than others should be encouraged through an award system. Staff promotions are a good incentive, as is national recognition or decoration. These incentives would discourage the traditional practice of only compensating academic qualifications and service records.

Even the scriptures recognize the importance of rewards. In Jude 1:20-21 believers are reminded to wait for the mercy of the Lord Jesus Christ for the eternal life.

The importance of targets is well known to those working in finance departments of the public service. Public expenditure budgets are targets, and these are popular and sought after goals. Funding is based on approved budgets which become performance targets. In this regard, no one can dispute the benefits realized from the wider application of the targets at the diplomatic missions. The present situation in which diplomatic missions have to seek guidance and approval on almost everything amounts to a wastage of time and resources. The introduction of targets to the other activities at the diplomatic missions would inevitably result in improved resources productivity. Creativity amongst the diplomatic staff would also be improved.

Demonstrable evidence has now been presented showing that without planning, the process of decision making is incapacitated. Good decisions are based on facts. Faith in the Lord Jesus Christ helps in making good decisions. While targets are easy to set when there is quantifiable production, it is not equally easy to establish similar targets in service industries. This is probably one of the reasons the diplomatic service has not benefited from the widespread application of targets. The pre-condition for the devolution of responsibility and accountability to the lowest level is the competence to make good decisions.

John Chikago

REFERENCES:

Mullins. L. (1996) – Management and Organizational Behavior,
4th Edition
London, Pitman Publishing

Ranson. S/Stewart. J [1994] – Management for the Public
Domain
Hong Kong,

Quinn. J [1998] – The Strategy Concept,
1st Edn, Great Britain
Prentice HALL

David. F [1998] – Strategic Management
7th Edn,
USA
Prentice Hall

Johnson. G/ Scholes. K [1997] – Exploring Corporate Strategy,
4th Edn, Hertfordshire, Hp 7EZ
Prentice Hall

Bennett. R [1994] – Effective Management,
The Kogan Page Guide,
1st Edition, Kogan Page Limited,
London NI 9JN

CHAPTER FOUR:

FUNDING TO DIPLOMATIC MISSIONS

The Bible is clear on the question of fair compensation. 1 Timothy 5:17-18 speaks about the importance of honoring good workers, including farm animals. As representative offices in foreign countries, diplomatic missions operate on funding from their home governments. Funds have to be made available for the diplomatic missions to pay service providers and living allowances. Without adequate funding, diplomatic missions are restricted as to what they can achieve. Therefore, the maintenance of diplomatic missions is a strategic decision.

It is easier to open than to close a diplomatic mission. The decision to open or close a mission is based upon cost benefit analysis. Oftentimes the high operating costs associated with the maintenance of diplomatic missions tend to overwhelm common sense, although citizens may be satisfied with the manner in which a particular diplomatic mission is managed.

But life is full of contradictions, and the consensus of negative opinion against one public function has created the impression that there is something wrong in the way in which the diplomatic missions are managed. Consequently, governments have been left with no alternative but to treat funding to diplomatic missions with extreme caution. The major problem arises from current funding arrangements. Funding to diplomatic missions is made in convertible currencies such as the American dollar. With the deteriorating terms of trade, the economies of most developing countries have become too weak to sustain exchange control transactions. One funding instruction to diplomatic missions may drain almost all the foreign reserves available to the country, depriving the private sector of the foreign currency needed for the importation of spare parts and raw materials.

The economies of the developing countries continue to deteriorate as world commodity prices remain depressed. Every time there is a devaluation of the local currency, the corresponding value of the hard currency increases. While the amount of foreign currency being externalized may remain unchanged, the corresponding amounts in the local currencies increase threefold, creating inflationary pressures throughout the country. Accordingly, more money has to be collected by increasing both direct and indirect taxes. Citizens then complain against the rising taxes which increase their cost of living. This is why the diplomatic missions have become the first target for public criticism.

There is specific legislation in every country that governs public revenue collection and expenditure. One such law requires all public revenue and expenditure estimates to be approved in plenary by legislative assemblies. The estimates for funding to diplomatic missions are also approved during the same time. With the consolidation of multiparty democracy in developing countries, the approval process has become a hard-selling job by those departments responsible for the management of public revenues. Approval must be obtained from the legislature after mounting a strong defense against opposition from elected representatives.

However, requesting increased funding levels is difficult to justify against competing public demands. Practically, public revenue trends are shrinking every year in real terms. Apart from low commodity prices, market liberalization has also stifled tax revenues from import duties and personal incomes. Domestic production and consumption have also suffered considerably due to the closure of many businesses. In this regard, there is no way a responsible legislature can approve public expenditure estimates to maintain diplomatic missions requiring half the total public revenue, especially when there is disagreement over operational status. Common sense dictates that diplomacy is not a pro-poor activity. Nor is it classified as an economic activity in the context of development diplomacy. The general perception is that of a state apparatus.

Obviously, there is divergence of opinion between governments and their citizens on this issue. It is disheartening to note that in spite of the overwhelming importance of development diplomacy, the actual role of the diplomatic missions is in a quagmire. Consequently, funding to the diplomatic missions continues to be a sensitive issue. Those authorizing funding may be treated as if they were committing a crime.

This misconception has to be resolved in order to create and maintain efficient operations of the diplomatic missions. In the same way a commercial farmer cannot cultivate the land without a tractor, diplomatic missions cannot promote development diplomacy without adequate funding. The importance of proper funding is well known in the private sector as witnessed by the private sector's support to marketers. No half-hearted endeavors should be tolerated when conducting the promotion of development diplomacy.

Funding Decision Rules

Decision rules are guidelines. The use of the guidelines simplifies the process of decision making. As pointed out previously, the public sector is notorious for its over reliance on rules and procedures. At no time should guidelines be considered as substitutes for good decision making. Guidelines should be issued as a frame of reference for decision making. Nevertheless, guidelines allow for consistency when treating expenses and enforcing discipline. Therefore, guidelines are important when allocating funding. Without the guidelines, it would not be possible to decide on levels of reasonable funding. It follows that the efficient allocation of public resources to diplomatic missions requires decision rules.

All things being equal, there should not be any need for decision rules. It is when demand exceeds the available resources that the decision rules become necessary. The precondition for efficient resource allocation is a clear purpose statement. The purpose statement will give a general view of the reason for the continued existence and rationale of the diplomatic mission. As discussed in the preceding chapter, the purpose statement should be supported by a list of operating objectives revealing ways in which the intended purpose would be achieved. This would provide a verifiable basis for funding. In the absence of the purpose statement and operating objectives, funding would be based solely on an individual's whims.

When allocating funding to diplomatic missions, it is wrong to treat them on the established concepts of equality of nation states. The equality of nation states is based on international conventions regarding territorial integrity and sovereignty. After the examination of a number of purpose statements, it becomes obvious that some states are more strategic than others.

Based on the strategic importance of the states, it is not correct to treat all diplomatic missions equally. The allocation of public funds should be varied in accordance with the purpose and strategic objective being pursued. For instance some diplomatic missions are located in world market countries, while others are located in capitals hosting the headquarters of strategic multilateral institutions. Still others are located in capitals where large numbers of people spend their holidays overseas. In order to be effective, it is imperative to take all these factors into consideration when formulating the funding decisions rules.

No doubt this approach delineates the difference between developed and developing countries. The developed countries do not experience foreign exchange control problems. When funding their diplomatic missions, their focus is on relocating resources. This is because most of the developed countries own the convertible currencies. Developed countries face monetary exchange problems when the diplomatic mission they want to fund is located in another developed country with a stronger convertible currency. Sometimes hard currencies strengthen against one another. When the value of one hard currency strengthens against another, it is bad news for the developed countries involved, because they need more money to trade amongst themselves; this may fuel inflation worldwide.

The strengthening of hard currencies is devastating news to poor developing countries. Substantial amounts of local currencies are needed to buy the same amount of foreign currencies expected at diplomatic missions. This is often where the citizens misunderstand the funding to diplomatic missions. Ideally, by expecting to add more local currency to meet the rising values of a strengthening hard currency, even more serious economic problems arise. Foreign exchange inflation is triggered, and that impacts negatively on the prices of imported commodities, causing general inflation in the developing country. When inflation rises, the cost of living increases and citizens in the developing countries suffer. The best counter strategy for such poor developing countries is to quickly reduce funding levels, hoping that the situation will improve with time. Unfortunately, oftentimes the eagerly awaited foreign exchange improvement does not come due to the continued deterioration of terms of trade on the world market.

It is important for governments in developing countries to realize that diplomatic missions are showrooms. Oftentimes, a first impression is what makes the difference. Marketers know the importance of first impression. When a new product's presentation strategy is poor, customers are not attracted to the product. Sometimes, the impression is so bad that a negative impression is fostered to the extent of killing the product. Consequently, there can be no half measures when it comes to imaging of diplomatic missions. Atrill/ Mclaney [1997. p. 7] support this view by saying that it is vitally important for organizations to plan their future and have a clear objective of what they want to achieve. Of course, there is no way a government can establish an office in a foreign country without having a purpose for its continued existence. Slack et al [1998. p. 352] agree that all operations require planning and controlling, although the formalities and detail of the plans may differ. Funding should therefore be based on the purposes being pursued.

Irrespective of foreign exchange problems, it is counterproductive for diplomatic missions to be funded equally. At best the purpose of funding should be to provide the means for good performance. The principle of carrot and stick is based on monitoring of performance, with corresponding rewards for good and bad performance. The overall aim is to reinforce discipline. Unfortunately, most governments do not have transparent performance monitoring systems. Even when some diplomatic missions are performing poorly, nothing is done to improve the situation. Mullins [1996 .p. 485] challenges that tendency by advising that there has to be a relationship between effort expended and a subsequent reward. When employees are not rewarded for what they achieve, they lose the motivation to work hard and performance suffers. This is probably the main factor adversely affecting the expected performance.

Funding to diplomatic missions is a complex subject, and it has different implications between the developed and the developing countries. Understandably, citizens frequently lose control of their endocrine glands when the subject of diplomatic missions is discussed. It is not a matter of common sense but strategic considerations.

Expenditure Control

The provision of adequate funding without proper expenditure management is the same as not being funded. The problem with money is, there is never enough. Good planning balances resource availability against demands; this is important. Without planning there cannot be control. Before anything else, effective expenditure control requires classification.

Based on practical experience, expenditures at diplomatic missions can be divided into two groups; costs incurred as a result of policy, and operating costs. Regarding the former, all governments make policies on the expenditure of things like housing of diplomatic staff, health insurance, transport, utilities, food, school fees and holidays. Policy costs inevitably behave as fixed costs. Once the policy is made, the diplomatic mission cannot change it. When extended to staff, the policy costs are treated as entitlements.

Regarding operating costs, it is important to understand that they are variable by nature. Unless anchored, variable costs are bound to rise. Here again there is need for good judgment and decision making. Expenditure must be relative to the cost of living of the location. One thing not to be forgotten when looking at variable costs is to understand the core business of diplomatic missions. Like in the private sector, a distribution company will spend more money on transportation. A green tea processing factory will spend more money on electricity. A hotel will spend more money on public relations. Obviously, diplomatic missions will spend more money on relationships marketing. This is the acid test for the evaluation of performance. In other words, if the core business of an organization is distribution, it is not justifiable for the organization to spend more money on electricity.

For far too long, diplomatic missions have been left in helpless situations from the beginning of their initial operations. When opening a diplomatic mission, traditionally some governments send a team of officials from headquarters mandated with the purpose of acquiring property at the new mission location. Usually, the officials spend no less than two weeks scouting for the property. Because they are visiting a new country, much of their time is spent sight seeing and vacationing. No matter how experienced they may be back at home, they cannot be objective enough to make good choices.

At best, they collect biased information from hotel staff and taxi drivers on the cost of living for the location. This results in under stating the initial cost benchmarks on living allowances for their mission personnel. Based upon these wrong assumptions, the diplomatic mission may be hampered with unrealistic funding from the beginning. Conversely, if the cost information is exaggerated from the beginning, the funding government is penalized with high policy costs for future years. Some of the current policy costs at diplomatic missions reflect these irregularities. Because the decision to open a new diplomatic mission is usually made at the highest level, it justifies the implementation of such crude approach. This is because high level decisions are expected to be implemented without delays.

The best approach is to send the future First Secretary in advance to the new mission station in the capacity of Chargé d'affaires to identify the property. Ample time should be allowed; up to a month if necessary. On arrival, the Chargé d'affaires should be allowed to operate from a hotel while looking for a suitable residence for the ambassador designate. After the suitable official residence is identified, the Chargé d'affaires should be authorized to conduct a flag hoisting ceremony for the property to be used as an interim Chancery. Immediately after identifying the residential property, the Chargé d'affaires should be permitted to take temporary occupancy of one room. This would reduce the cost of living in the hotel until the arrival of the ambassador designate.

The difference between the two approaches is the preferred allocation of responsibility and accountability to an individual. The officer sent in advance would be more careful when making long term decisions because of undesired consequences. Conversely, there is no way a group of bureaucrats would take responsibility for one mistake. This is probably one of the reasons some policy costs have become prohibitive for the continued operation of some diplomatic missions. Undoubtedly some high policy costs reflect these initial mistakes. The practice of sending an army of officials to identify property at new mission stations is more expensive and less transparent. Also, all transactions made within this group approach are made in cash. This means trusting bureaucrats with public funds in their pockets.

In the second approach, at least some of the transactions can be conducted through the bank. One of the first assignments that the officer sent in advance should do is to open bank accounts with counter signatures obtained from diplomatic missions from friendly neighboring states if already in the country. Public expenditure operates on the principle of transparency. It is transparency that facilitates audit trails.

Property Ownership

Diplomats use many tools in the practice of their duties with the aim of translating words to action. Believers also use different means to spread the word of God. Some believers use the means of evangelism. Some use the means of fellowship. Others use the means of music. Obviously, there are many ways to spread the word of God. In diplomacy, one of the means is property ownership. This is a strategic decision which governments have to make. There is often a misconception that governments committing to property ownership have no financial problems. On the contrary, the decision to own property is a statement of commitment to the existing bilateral relations. No reasonable government can invest in a building if unsure of continuity. Many people in developing countries have no good houses in their villages because there is no market for rent in the villages. They have better houses in cities and towns for purposes of collecting high rentals.

Governments have to make the decision between renting or buying property within those countries their missions will be located. Owning property at mission locations cannot be generalized; there is need for the decision to be based on some guidelines. Begg et.al. [1994. p. 217] advise that acquisition of property should reflect cost benefits. By owning property, government acquires title to a future stream of capital service the property would intrinsically be providing. It is clear, therefore, that property ownership by governments provide diplomatic mission with future cost advantages. It is important to undertake a cost benefit analysis in a form of balance sheet before taking the decision between buying and renting property. With the never ending liquidity problems facing many developing countries, the best choice is to aim at owning property, preferably in locations with high rental values. Owning property in such expensive places will offer dividends from the reduced effects of future increases of property values.

Where the cost of living is low and diplomatic relations are not as strategic, it is advisable to rent or lease property. The same strategy should apply to discretionary items such as office equipment and transportation. It is wrong to aim for owning everything at the diplomatic mission. Why? Office equipment is difficult to change when owned, and it creates problems when new office technology is introduced. In the case of motor vehicles, it would be cost effective for the cars at the diplomatic missions to be replaced on the expiration of the manufacturer's warranty because warranty reflects the economic life of the car. The expiration of the manufacturer's warranty marks the beginning of a physical life that is associated with frequent "wear and tear" maintenance costs.

The time has come when diplomatic missions should be managed as business institutions. It is not right for governments to advocate development diplomacy when the management culture is left unchanged.

The Cost of Bank Services

Banks make money from managing money transactions. In other words, no bank can survive without dealing in money. All transactions at commercial banking institutions cost money, and those costs involve recovery risks and administration. When banks receive foreign funds, they charge fees for the transaction. Similarly, when making payments to service providers through a checking account, the bank charges a fee to recover its costs.

There is overwhelming evidence that some diplomatic missions have become sources of huge income for some commercial banks. In spite of the high banking charges, some governments seem to insensitively continue with banking practices that impact negatively on public revenue.

Governments traditionally fund diplomatic missions on a monthly basis so as to consistently maintain those budgets with other publicly funded functions. Unlike domestic transactions which are unaffected by the fluctuating values of foreign currencies, the remittances to diplomatic missions are vulnerable. Every month the value of the foreign currency is changing. Governments could conceivably save substantial amounts of money if remittances to diplomatic missions were transacted in a different way. Results of a recent academic research by Chikago [2000. p. 23] indicated that out of fifty-three governments sampled in developing countries, only 15% funded their diplomatic missions on a monthly basis. The overwhelming majority, equal to 65% of the governments, funded their diplomatic missions on a quarterly basis. Also emerging from the academic research was the fact that 15% of the governments funded their missions biannually. The remaining 5% funded their diplomatic missions on an impress basis. The funding by impress transfers the responsibility of financial management and accountability to the ambassador.

Why is it that some governments do not externalize the funds when the foreign exchange situations are favorable? The answer is often not clear. Such tendencies make the operations of the public service unattractive. Generally, the attitude is to avoid taking responsibility by making reference to speculations and unrealistic conclusions. When suggestions for change of the systems are made, the usual excuse is that it is against public service regulations. And yet the public service is a trust for all citizens. The public employees, commonly known as civil servants, are trustees who are paid for working on behalf of the citizens. This includes the elected representatives, who are also trustees on behalf of the citizens. Who then would introduce the changes? This is the dilemma that stalls progress and hampers resource productivity in the public service.

It is needless to conclude that the introduction of a new way of thinking is an immediate priority for the status quo in the public service to change. While parliaments approve the revenue and expenditure budgets that are used to run public businesses, there is need to change the management practices in government. Employees at diplomatic missions should be given the power of decision making. It is unreasonable to expect anything good from employees who do not apply judgments to their jobs. The new way should also include discussions by parliaments on expenditure systems. Instead of only checking audited reports presented by the Auditor General's office, the parliaments should also examine expenditure systems in general, including funding procedures. Clearly large amounts of money are lost through foreign exchange transactions at commercial banks. It may be advisable for governments to hedge against virulent foreign exchange movements by investing forward when the foreign exchange situations are favorable.

<u>REFERENCES:</u>

Atrill/McLaney.E [1997.] – Accounting and Finance
for Non-Specialists
2nd Edition, Great Britain,
Prentice Hall

Slack.N et al [1998] – Operations Management
2nd Edition, UK
Pitman Publishing.

Chikago.J [2000] – Master of Business Administration Thesis
Pretoria, South Africa.

CHAPTER FIVE:

RELATIONSHIP MARKETING IN DIPLOMACY

To Christian believers, relationship marketing could be described as fellowship. Psalms 133:1 hails the importance of believers living together in harmony. Warren [2003. p. 139] explains that in real fellowship, people experience authenticity. When people share authentic relationships, the outcome is genuine heart to heart feelings. Warren further argues that in real fellowship, there is mutuality. Using geometric language, one would say in real fellowship, there is congruency. When people experience a mutuality of ideas, they share consensus on many things. In that way, they feel empathy for one another. When one has a problem, it becomes the problem for all members in the group.

Relationship marketing is a process of building networks and business coalitions. It is not selling, but rather the process of winning friends. Similarly, the promotion of development diplomacy is a relationship marketing exercise. It revolves around the cultivation of good interpersonal relations. The starting point for an effective relationship marketing process is good interpersonal skills. In that regard, the promotion of development diplomacy is impossible without the skills necessary for building interpersonal relationships.

Kotler [1996. p. 12] agrees by explaining that relationship marketing is the process of building long term mutually beneficial personal relationships. The adoption of this statement is necessary, as the establishment of diplomatic relations is generally the result of good inter-personal relations between two Heads of State.

It is therefore reasonable to conclude that the establishment of diplomatic relations manifests the level of commitment to friendship between two Heads of State. Additionally, there are many other ways in which commitment to bilateral relations between two friendly countries could be demonstrated. There is the exchange of high level visits; the giving of economic aid in the form of official development assistance; supporting one another on critical issues at the United Nations General Assembly. Ownership of property is another powerful demonstration of commitment to bilateral relations. Property such as a building is an immovable asset and it costs substantial amounts of money. Therefore, the decision to own property in foreign capitals is a serious commitment to diplomatic relations.

Some wealthier countries even go as far as subsidizing rental expenses for poor countries in financial distress to show commitment to bilateral relations. Such developments prove beyond reasonable doubt that with diplomacy, actions speak louder than words. It is more than the rhetoric expressed through the press. However, there is the need to ensure that the actions are proportionate and relative to avoid wastage of resources

The conceptualization of the world as a global village has underlined the importance of demonstrating the correct symbols of commitment to bilateral relations. Kotler [1996. p. 2] warns that with the demise of the Cold War and the subsequent spread of democracy in developing countries, the world wrestles with ruthless competition and serious economic gaps. Small countries are now competing with big countries for investments. What initially seemed like a plethora of opportunities in the horizons of change have become heartbreaking challenges. Subsequently, pragmatic diplomacy has been infiltrated by cross cultural influences, making the use of marketing tools more imperative.

However, conducting relationship marketing is as complicated as the marketing of any tangible product. When potential investors treat all countries equally, the ability to develop country specific differentiation strategies is a key success factor. The need to use suitable differentiation strategies is therefore a precondition for the establishment of regional economic groupings aimed at harmonizing markets. Without adopting the correct strategic differentiation, only a few countries will emerge as winners from the market multilateralism inherent in the global village.

Differentiation refers to the crafting of winning strategies. When all countries are considered equally on the basis of democratic governance, it is difficult for investors to decide where to invest and for tourists to choose where to spend their holidays. The private sector is good at creating perceptual identities for their companies. These are the identities which individual countries pursuing development diplomacy are expected to project. For example, a landlocked country can project the image of a cheap regional distribution centre; a country that is endowed with indigenous forests can project itself as a centre for the research of medicinal plants; another country can position itself as the transit hub for tourists. All these identities are strategic postures enabling individual countries to define their desired perceptual identities.

Although relationship marketing helps a country to create an identity for potential investors to study and assess, it is important to note that the effort is expensive. According to Kotler [1996. p. 48-52], relationship marketing is expensive when conducting initial negotiations. The first process is that of identifying potential investors. The process involves a variety of initiatives and pragmatic assessments.

The challenge is how to overcome cultural differences. Business cultures differ from country to country. In some business cultures, it is not the company president who makes the investment decisions. It could be some junior clerk in a strategic department shielded from public attention. The problem is where or how to start. This is probably the process that is expensive because it involves a discovery period; underpinning the importance of resource availability.

This means that diplomatic missions must have unflinching support in order to succeed in their efforts. It is disheartening when bureaucrats, some of whom have never served in the diplomatic service, believe that development diplomacy can be promoted without adequate resources. This is the operational challenge most diplomatic missions confront. Pursuing development diplomacy without adequate monetary support is like squeezing blood from a stone. Undoubtedly this is the attitude that has contributed to the mediocrity and poor performances of some of the diplomatic missions. Development diplomacy is expensive therefore cannot succeed without adequate funding.

Unless the staffs at the diplomatic missions are able to convert potential investors to prospective investors, the rest of the effort becomes a waste of time and resources. The process of confidence building is a mixed bag of mutually reinforcing initiatives, some of which are reactive rather than proactive. The outcome of the whole process should culminate in the winning of personal friends adding to the mission's professional network. Many times these friendships and networks develop advocates who are prepared to endorse and promote a country publicly and privately.

The relationships developed transcend from friendship to partnership. Almost always, potential investors prefer to be treated as partners, and a country referring to them as such encourages expeditious investment decisions.

Differentiation Strategy

The foregoing defines the process of relationship marketing as the motivating force behind the success of development diplomacy. Evidence is available that relationship marketing is misunderstood as any meeting between the private and public sector. Relationship marketing is a meeting between people who are interested to break social distances and work as close friends. Obviously, diplomatic missions have complicated assignments on their hands. The promotion of development diplomacy inevitably is a variable of resource availability and differentiation strategies. Without adequate resources and appropriate differentiation strategies, diplomatic missions cannot achieve anything. Any effort they make without balancing the two is like chasing the wind.

Differentiation strategies enable diplomatic missions to build perceptual identities of their respective countries. These identities help potential investors to develop positive images of those countries. Again it is a chicken and egg situation. There is no way the investor can make an investment decision to a country before the relations have developed to the level of friendship and trust. Prevailing cultural differences dictate the type of relationship marketing initiative to be used. A social event planned for one country based upon cultural influences may not be practical for another country.

Just as individual people are different, communities also have different cultures. Some communities promote independent living in which case the interest of the individual family is more important than that of the community as a whole. In these communities, the power of the individual is valued over that of the group. Relationship marketing is easy to implement in such communities. In these communities, usually what matters most at the end of the day is what the individual gains personally. The only disadvantage of communities influenced by the individual culture is corruption.

On the other hand, there are some communities which promote and favor group cultures. It is the power of the group as opposed to that of the individual members that matters. Consequently, the conduct of relationship marketing is not as complicated in the communities practicing group cultures as it is in the case in the communities motivated by individual cultures mentioned above. The group culture is common in Asia, and this may be one of the reasons South East Asian countries have witnessed rapid economic development within a short period of time. Obviously, the group approach minimizes the probability of greed, the root cause of corruption.

The importance of adopting the correct relationship marketing initiatives when promoting development diplomacy cannot be overemphasized due to the striking differences between the two cultures described above. Group cultures would suit the hosting of cocktail parties, while luncheons and dinners would suit those cultures that empower individuals.

There is understandably a critical need to undertake comprehensive studies on business cultures in different countries before embarking on any promotional efforts.

Some governments fail to appreciate the existence of the cultural differences by treating all diplomatic missions equally on the basis of public sector ethical considerations of equality, fairness and consistency. The nondiscriminatory tendencies may have contributed to the current performance problems. Unfortunately, not many citizens may have the knowledge of the disabling factors being faced by their diplomatic missions. Consequently, the problem of poor performance of the diplomatic missions is often assigned to the staff. Without power to make decisions, it is unfair for the staff to be assigned the blame. Here again the point to remember is that responsibility and accountability must always correspond.

As is true with any form of marketing, relationship marketing inevitably is a long term process; it does not yield immediate results. What is required is continuity of effort. It must be incremental and persistent. Relationship marketing is like saving for the future – today's marketing efforts will pay dividends in the future. It should therefore be treated in the same manner as the public sector treats infrastructure development. Rural crop extraction roads are usually built before farmland is cultivated. Ironically, there is need for a *long-term* approach to development diplomacy. Development diplomacy should be apolitical if it has to make the difference.

The foregoing arguments create the impression that the high expectations of development diplomacy are being challenged. Bureaucrats and elected representatives have added to these expectations by promising citizens improved results from diplomatic missions on the premise of switching from the promotion of political interests to development diplomacy. As with all things, the precondition for success is planning. It is when planning and reviewing fundamental issues that deficiencies and shortcomings will be exposed. As of now, the yardsticks for measuring the performance of diplomatic missions are varied and subjective.

Cross Sector Influence

Understandably, the challenges facing the management of diplomatic missions are many. Pressure from the public is intensifying daily in an unprecedented way. There is total confusion on the best way diplomatic missions are expected to operate. Some believe that with the transformation from political to economic diplomacy, the diplomatic missions should be managed by the private sector. Such a view may not be feasible owing to the inherent privileges enjoyed by the diplomatic missions, arising from their subscriptions to international conventions.

One would like to think that those members of the public advancing such views are confusing with the operations of consular offices. Consular offices have different operational mandates to those of diplomatic missions. This is why the latter usually functions as a joint partnership between the private and public sectors.

In most countries, consular offices are jointly funded and managed by the two sectors. In that regard, the hiring of employees to work at the consular offices is also expected to be a joint exercise.

This is not the case with diplomatic missions. The diplomatic missions can only change the policy over staff recruitment by maintaining a mixture of skills with the aim of achieving a strategic fit and synergy.

Indeed, one of the benefits brought by democracy is the public sector's ability to transfer some of its responsibilities to the private sector. The public sector has also been able to emulate some of the procedures and practices of the private sector. This is why some citizens are not able to appreciate the fundamental differences between the two sectors. However, some of the cross functional influences have created new challenges along the line. Fig. 1 shows the perceived operational area of consular offices.

Fig.1

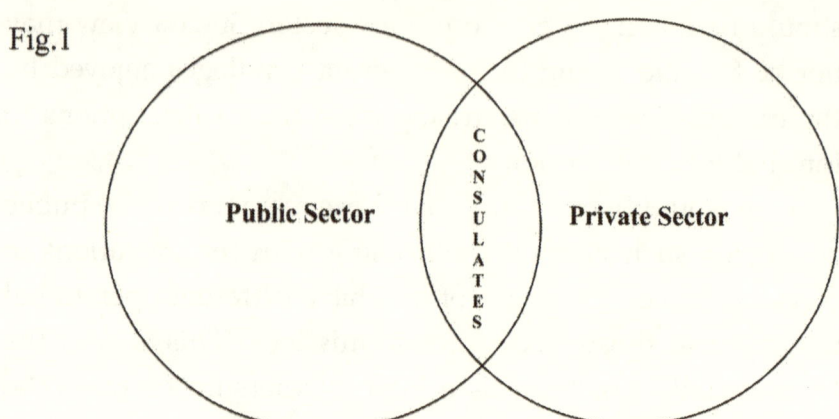

There is no way diplomatic missions can operate on the periphery of private sector business, and it is wrong to assume that the introduction of development diplomacy will justify the violation of diplomatic convections.

Intangible Commodity

Marketing involves the promotion of two types of products. The first type of product is physical in character; it is tangible and felt. The marketing of physical products is easier because there are samples to show. Prospective customers have the opportunity to touch, feel and taste the product.

The second type of product is services. Services are intangible and difficult to market because no one can see them. Service is like the Christian faith – faith cannot be displayed. Hebrews 11:1-2 says faith is described as being sure of what cannot be seen. Christians believe the universe was formed at God's command, so that what is seen was made out of what was invisible.

The same applies to diplomatic service – no one can see it. People talk about diplomatic service without physically displaying it. Similarly, development diplomacy is intangible. No one can see development diplomacy. Diplomats can only talk about it in abstract terms. This view underlines the importance of creating country identities. Every country that is determined to promote development diplomacy has to start by creating its own national identity. The question to answer is why the investor should come and invest in the country and not in the neighboring one? Why the tourist should visit the country and not the neighboring one? Those are the type of questions to be answered when crafting a country's national identity.

In all this, the precondition is the ability to conduct constructive self criticisms. When undertaking the identity creation exercise, functional efforts must be mutually reinforcing for the foreigners to develop the correct image. Elements of lack of functional cooperation militate against the confidence of foreigners interested to visit the country. When foreigners are visiting a country for the first time, they should be treated well in order for them not to lose the image, they held for the country.

Like marketers, diplomatic missions use social occasions to promote investments, tourism and trade. There is no better substitute for the process of marketing intangible products than building confidence through social interactions.

Whereas it is easier to sell a packet of tea, it is not the same with development diplomacy. When all countries are treated equally for sharing the common values of democracy, it is incumbent upon every diplomatic mission to market its home country through a differentiation strategy. Obviously, the strategy of differentiation is easier to implement on physical products. The products are differentiated in many ways: color, smell, size and shape. Differentiation strategies for the promotion of development diplomacy are not so easy to implement.

Therefore it is mere opportunism to expect diplomatic missions to realize results without the provision of the necessary resources. Such expectations only help to prove that developing countries will not get much from the innovation. What must be appreciated is that developed countries which are cooperating partners to most developing countries are also competing for foreign direct investments by offering the availability of skilled human resource, large consumer markets, and the advantages of advanced technologies such as the computer. Obviously only resource seeking investments would be attracted to the developing countries, and that is why it is important to carefully construct and develop national identities that would project a country's specific comparative advantages.

It is not merely a matter of providing resources at the diplomatic mission. Each mission location should be chosen on the basis of strategic interests. For instance, diplomatic missions which are located primarily for political interests should not be judged to have failed to promote development diplomacy. Those diplomatic missions promote peace and stability, which are prerequisites to economic development.

To reiterate, this is why the careful preparation of purpose statements would be beneficial when making strategic decisions. People only give what they have. Similarly, countries only give what they have. For instance, it is unreasonable to expect economic assistance from other aid receiving countries. Development diplomacy is not a magic wand which can make impossibilities become possibilities.

Development diplomacy has evolved and is now an international issue. To the developing countries it is an innovation, but not to the developed countries. Since ancient times, the developed countries have always pursued development diplomacy. In fact, the colonial enterprise was a development diplomacy program as its main aim was to look for cheap raw materials from foreign countries. The industrial revolution was the precursor to the flow of foreign direct investments to poor countries during that time. To the contrary, the poor countries did not do anything to promote the foreign direct investment as is the case now.

At last, every developing country has embraced the concept of development diplomacy as the means of promoting trade and investments for ending underdevelopment and poverty.

Naturally, the allocation of monthly funding to diplomatic missions should be based on what is to be achieved. It costs money to make money. A six cylinder car engine cannot work on fuel intended for a one cylinder engine. Therefore, funding decisions should be guided by strategic considerations

It is important that diplomatic missions portray the identities of their home countries. And the projection of the identities should be an on-going national issue. Relationship marketing would succeed only when those identities are crafted.

Some developing countries have the belief of projecting poverty when promoting development diplomacy. The leaders of such countries would better be politely advised that the perception and reaction to poverty situations vary from person to person. For instance, some people abstain from associating with poverty stricken countries. Such people are not interested in visiting countries that are ravaged by poverty for reasons known to themselves. Many citizens in developing countries blame the international media for misinformation and negative press coverage of their countries.

In reality, the deliberate statements by some leaders from the poor countries contribute to the problem.

Poverty cannot and will never be a comparative advantage. Everyone knows that poverty exacerbates criminality.

While modern technology has achieved tremendous advancements in communication through the use of the Internet, the benefits and effects of conducting business on face to face basis remains unsurpassed. Potential tourists want to listen to personal testimonies from those who have visited this or that country. Merely reading brochures does not provide the same experience. Therefore, many foreigners do not believe the printed brochures. This emphasizes the importance of providing diplomatic missions with adequate resources to host receptions and National Day celebrations, regardless of the economic conditions. When such events take place, it is relationship marketing at its best. The public sector needs to rethink and appreciate the concept of relationship marketing. The performance of diplomatic missions will definitely improve when relationship marketing is incorporated into the public sector as a management strategy.

The Human Face
of Development Diplomacy

Having discussed the importance of relationship marketing for the implementation of development diplomacy, it is imperative to look at the type of people to be recruited for the job. When addressing the question, it is necessary to avoid the temptation of forgetting or ignoring what the scriptures say about human creation; the scriptures are clear when it comes to the creation of human beings. Every human being was created in the image of God with a specific purpose. Warren [2002. p. 17] argues that the search for purpose has been a difficult matter because of human weakness.

Usually, when identifying potential candidates for the diplomatic appointments, some people assume the role of God. No wonder that diplomacy has not been useful to citizens. Unless the recruitment exercise is guided by God, nothing good would be achieved by those appointed to serve.

It is true that different people have different abilities. Unless specific tasks are implemented by people with abilities, nothing would ever be achieved. What type of people should serve at the diplomatic missions? The first part of the answer has already been provided. Everything must start in God. Political diplomacy bordered on intelligence gathering; consequently, the job required programmed human minds. That was one of the reasons career diplomacy became an important tool. Certainly the promotion of trade, tourism, investments and economic assistance does not require the involvement of human machines as was the case during the Cold War.

Development diplomacy requires level-headed people who appreciate that every country was created by God before they were created. Human beings only became inhabitants of the individual countries at God's pleasure. In that respect there is no one country which is better to God. All countries are the same to God. The relative material differences are man-made. Any country can change its material wealth with faith in God. Therefore, the people to be appointed should therefore have the heart to serve others and not themselves.

Exodus 18:21 advises those who serve others should fear God, be trustworthy and hate dishonest gains.

Appointees must also have different professional backgrounds for the diplomatic mission to benefit from synergy of ideas. The ones with relevant experience in trade, tourism, defense, security, economics, production, parliamentary politics, teaching, and even sports should be selected primarily on their ability to promote development diplomacy. The precondition is to identify strategic interests in the country of assignment in order to achieve a calculated fit with staff backgrounds.

Therefore, the introduction of development diplomacy should not create unnecessary confusion among decision makers. It is not a job for angels nor is it a job for saints. It is a national service for citizens who know God and have knowledge of how the world was created. Deep in their minds they have to realize that public service is a clarion call to the country's citizens. As civil servants, they are employees of the citizens. They have to understand that government is a national and sacred trust for the citizens.

REFERENCES:

Silbiger. S [1994] – THE 10-DAY MBA
                    2nd Edition, Judy Piatkus Publishing Ltd,
                    London, United Kingdom.

Warren.R [2003] – The Purpose Driven Life
                    Purpose-Driven Ministries, Philippines

Kotler.P [1997] – Marketing Management, 9th Edition
                    Prentice Hall International Inc.
                    New Jersey
                    U.S.A.

CHAPTER SIX:

DEVELOPMENT DIPLOMACY

Development diplomacy means the promotion of economic interests by diplomatic missions. The Cold War situation simplified the practice of diplomacy with the diplomatic staff spending most of their time on unproductive issues. The promotion of economic interests was not part of their responsibility. The giving of Official Development Assistance [ODA] was a matter of identifying with a political ideology. The mere presence of a diplomatic mission was sufficient to earn recognition for the award of the Cold War spoils. With its demise in 1993, an avalanche of political buzzwords such as development diplomacy, governance, accountability and responsibility have all become part of diplomatic vocabulary.

As always, the danger of buzzwords is that they have different interpretations. Their inconsistent meanings tend to act as fuel for mass psychology.

No wonder that suddenly the term "development diplomacy" has been popularized to the point of losing meaning. Over usage of the term has left an optimistic impression that the end of poverty is within reach. When citizens are told about the change to development diplomacy, they become elated, nobly persevering for the day when their living standards will also change for the better.

Obviously, this is a wrong message to people who are suffering from poverty. The right message is for the people to have faith in God, the Creator of all things. The story about development diplomacy and its potential to improve the economic situation has no value to them. It is better to advise them to place their hope in God and discover His gifts by reading the scriptures. It is only through faith in God that lasting solutions to poverty will be found. Jeremiah 9: 23-24 warns against men who boast without understanding, and knowing God as the Lord.

Political systems cannot provide the solutions to poverty. The problem with political systems is with the leaders who champion them. Any political leadership not inspired by the power of faith is bound to fail as politics is the process of governing oneself well before governing others. Some people go into politics to govern others, not themselves. Kim [1984. p. 204] argues that a good leader should have an exemplary lifestyle.

There is also the notion that economic development will be realized through the efforts of foreign investors. Would the foreign investors come as philanthropists? If that is the expectation, then it is necessary to state that it is wrong. First, the foreign investors are human beings. They have their own home countries where they can invest their money safely. As human beings, they are influenced by many factors including emotions.

The first factor is that of fear. When mentioning fear, an immediate temptation is to ascribe it to crime rate. Unfortunately, the crime rate is not always a critical factor when making investment decisions. There is contemporary evidence proving that crime is not the critical issue influencing investment decisions. The risks of crime are often outweighed by the strategic nature of the investment opportunity. However, some investors feel safer when dealing with people of faith.

The other factor influencing investment decisions is the availability of local partners. If a country has no evidence of local direct investment, it is difficult if not impossible for it to attract foreign direct investments. All things being equal, foreign direct investment follows local direct investments. It is like the saying: "one good turn deserves another." Unless citizens have stakes in local investments, it is unlikely for foreign investors to come.

Therefore, in the absence of local equity participation the attraction of foreign capital is highly improbable owing to lack of comparative database on which to make investment decisions. There is an honest but wrong belief in developing countries of publishing beautiful brochures as the means for promoting foreign investments. Unless combined with other initiatives, the brochures can be a waste of money. It is unlikely that foreign investors will be attracted by the circulation of the brochures alone.

———

Admittedly, diplomacy has become complicated in recent years. A myriad of yardsticks have been developed for the evaluation of performance of diplomatic mission.

Simultaneously, pressure against increased funding has also intensified from citizens. The citizens as is their right are concerned about value for money. They want to be assured that the pursuance of development diplomacy by the diplomatic mission will someday bring positive changes to their lives. As indicated earlier on, when such debates are taking place, the hope is not in God but political systems. The reality is that man-made systems without God's blessings are doomed to fail, and citizens will be left worse off than before. Matthew 7:11 says the Father in heaven gives good gifts to those who ask him.

Leadership without Responsibility

The consolidation of democracy in developing countries has also meant the entrenchment of market liberalization. Governments have lost the privilege of exercising partisan control over investment decisions as was the case before the introduction of democracy. In turn the private sector has assumed a leadership role on investment decisions while demand and supply forces control the markets. Sadly, the private sector has accepted its new role with half-measures, denying responsibility and accountability. It seems it has accepted a role it does not fully understand.

The evidence is when the occasion to promote investments and trade arises; the attitude of waiting for government to lead the way is unchanged. Subsequently, almost all investment promotional materials are published by the use of public funds. Surprisingly, the private sector is meekly heard invoking its leadership role as engine for economic growth at cocktail parties. A legitimate question is on the meaning of the leadership role when investment, trade and tourism promotional efforts continue to be made by governments?

This is a fundamental question because of the important catalytic role the private sector makes for the flow of foreign direct investment. It may not be wrong to conclude that some developing countries acted too quickly to embark on privatization of state assets. What is the benefit of privatization when public resources are still being used to promote investments? What is the value of privatization when citizens have no stakes in the privatized assets?

Effective privatization should have taken place after the establishment of land and property banks to mobilize domestic capital. The fact is that people in developing countries have dead capital hidden in land and buildings owing to the absence of the property and land banks. Evidence is plentiful that the success stories of some developed countries originated from the recognition of property and land values. When such property was given title by the specialized banks, the citizens of the countries were able to access investments capital. In hindsight, it is right to think that some of the privatization in most of the developing countries should have waited for the establishment of the facilitating institutions.

Now the situation has become a dilemma to all concerned. The absence of local direct investment is a serious challenge. The dearth of property and land banks means there is no reliable investment facilitating institutions for local equity participation. The capacity by governments to release catalytic funds for investments has been hamstrung by the effect of rushing privatization. Based on these developments, the best option left is to revitalize some of the strategic development institutions.

Before anything is done, though, there is need for moral regeneration. Citizens in the developing countries must accept the scriptures not as history but instruction for practical living. Nothing can be achieved without God's blessing. What is required is strong faith in the invisible God.

New Rules, Same Game

In recent years, new conditions for the flow of foreign direct investments have emerged. The first condition is availability of resources such as fossil oils, lumber, precious metals and fishing facilities.

Foreign capital for the procurement of these resources is available in the world. The second condition is availability of large markets; markets not only large in size, but also with the propensity to spend. The third condition for the flow of foreign capital is availability of skilled human resource. The last condition is availability of local capital for partnerships.

The recent investment criteria highlight the challenges facing developing countries in the globalizing market. Obviously, it will be a daunting task to promote development diplomacy in the absence of coordinated cross-functional approach. In the face of these challenges, it is advisable to conduct strategic reviews on country specific comparative advantages in order to attract the new forms of foreign direct investments.

Resource Seeking Foreign Investment

By God's purpose, many developing countries are endowed with abundant natural resources. The problem undermining the countries from deriving maximum benefits from their natural resources is right of ownership. The harmful legacies of colonialism continue to hinder the freedoms of ownership by the countries. Sadly, most of the countries sold the rights to their resources for short-term benefits during the colonial period. Consequently, the situation has become a mockery in that the rights to the resources are held elsewhere; proving that ownership and power of control cannot be separated.

The overwhelming majority of citizens in the countries continue to live as bewildered spectators to economic activities tilted in favor of foreigners. The resources are taken out in raw form, before adding value, making it impossible for the national economies to register fast growth. The same materials return to the developing countries as finished products at prices not affordable by ordinary citizens. Undoubtedly, this contributes to the poverty adversely affecting life in these countries. In this context, the developing countries are donors of strategic resources at unrealistic prices. It is not wrong to assume that the international community has a moral obligation to reverse the current situation. This is where the power of faith in leadership is hoped to bring fairness to the trading systems in the world. Understandably, the situation cannot be resolved by the leaders who are not inspired by the power of faith.

The world commodity trade provides a good starting point when discussing businesses that benefit foreign interests. It is important to remember that the aim of introducing crops such as tea, sugar, tobacco and coffee in developing countries by the colonial enterprise was a sourcing strategy. Increased consumption made it an imperative for the colonial empire to look for cheap sources of the commodities. It is not, therefore, taking political sides to state that the commodity trade today is the continuation of an antiquated colonial economic constitution designed to provide backward linkages to foreign consumer markets.

The aim at the time was not to benefit the local economies. Again, these views should not be construed as demeaning the social and economic contributions which were made by the colonial investments. There is no question that the primary industries created jobs, foreign currency and tax revenue. The point at issue is not about jobs – it is the unfair trading terms which are now creating mixed feelings among the poor people living in these countries.

One thing for a fact is that the jobs were not offered for charity. Workers in the plantations should have been considered as factors of production. Without the workers there could not be production. It is true that some owners of the resource seeking capital are not interested in the history of investments; all they want are the resources. In their thinking, the marketing problems should have been addressed at the time of attaining national independence. On the contrary, most of the nationalist leaders at independence were preoccupied by the desire to muster unfettered political power. Where attempts were made to gain economic power, the option was nationalization programs.

Some of the nationalist leaders also embarked on unplanned import substitution programs. Unfortunately, both nationalistic economic experiments failed with disastrous results. The liabilities for some of the mistakes have been passed on to posterity through high inflation, poor living standards and meaningless life.

The other problem some developing countries are facing is that of production capacity. The production capacity for some of the important primary products such as coffee, tea, macadamia nuts is too small to meet international consumer demands of large markets. Most of the countries are in pilot stages of production. The crops they claim to produce cannot even fill five twenty-foot containers.

How then, would the introduction of development diplomacy solve these tactical challenges? Unless the capacity problems are addressed, development diplomacy would only become another scapegoat.

While the resource seeking foreign capital is abundantly available, it is high time for the developing countries to identify and partner with friendly developed countries; not just all developed countries. One important point to consider is that some developed countries look at developing countries as burdens, while others view them as strategic partners. As discussed earlier, some developed nations have selfish cultures in which the individual is viewed as more important than the group. Investors from such cultures should be dealt with cautiously due to their dangerous cultural paradigms of greed. This means that the tendency of giving equal importance to foreign investor should be reviewed.

Market Seeking Foreign Investments

Some foreign investors have capital for countries with large markets. It is not just the population size that counts, but its propensity to spend. The question here concerns money in the pockets of citizens. This may be the reason some regional markets in developing countries are failing to achieve the purpose for which they were established. With this observation, it is necessary to admit that it will take time for some developing countries to become attractive destinations for the market seeking foreign investments. Obviously, the potential destinations for such investment capital are developed countries. This is where the promotion of development diplomacy becomes a complex matter. Balancing competitive interests between rich and poor countries cannot be a simple matter.

It is important to appreciate that the propensity to spend is associated with economic growth. The precondition for economic growth is productivity improvement. High productivity can be realized when every citizen works hard. National economic growth cannot be achieved by the importation of ready-made goods. Ideally the importation of ready-made goods has the same devastating effect as the exportation of primary goods. This is probably one of the reasons the economies of the developing countries are failing to register meaningful growth rates. Food insecurity is another problem stifling economic growth. When a country depends on imported staple food, consumer inflation becomes uncontrollable. The threshold for national economic growth is surplus food production.

In an effort to generate disposable incomes, some developing countries embarked on market led economies before putting in place the necessary legal and economic infrastructure. Subsequently, the macro-economic exercise stifled the meager production that was taking place, causing high unemployment rates and runaway inflation. Practical experience has shown that market liberalization does not protect inefficient businesses. It sets out a virulent business environment in which only the best managed businesses survive. This is not to say that market liberalization is bad;

it aims at releasing efficiency through market competition. However, its introduction demands strategic planning coupled with common sense.

In this regard, few developing countries will benefit from the market seeking investments. This investment is flowing very fast within the developed countries. It is not a conspiracy, but simply market forces at work. The best course left for developing countries is to concentrate on using what God gave them; land, minerals, coastal lines teeming with tasty fish, lumber, fossil oils and strong bodied people. It makes no sense to sulk on what God did not give the country. Every resource available in a country has God's purpose. The scriptures in James 1: 5 advise those lacking wisdom to pray to God, who gives it generously and graciously.

Skill Seeking Foreign Investments

Other owners of foreign capital are anxious to invest in countries where skilled human resources are in abundance. The type of skills available in a particular country is an attraction to these investors. The skill seeking investment is sometimes known as efficiency seeking investment. It has three main objectives. The first objective is to benefit from high productivity levels; the second objective is to win the competition through high quality products, and the third objective is to become price leaders for the products in the world market. In a world where product competition is high, success is achieved through cost leadership and quality. This is a popular strategy regarding high technology products such as computer hardware and software and electronic assembly lines.

Obviously, any developing country hoping to attract the efficiency seeking investment has to nurture and foster an educational system that teaches market related skills. Therefore, it is advisable for governments in developing countries to implement strategic plans for national education, so that periodically comprehensive reviews are undertaken to evaluate the relevance of the system to skill development.

Usually, major problems derive from lack of coordination. It is not uncommon to find within the same government, different departments working at cross purposes without consultations. For instance, one government department might be pushing for tax remission while another is looking for increased public revenue. Similarly, another department might be looking for improvements to national security while yet another would be asking for increased budgetary allocation for the promotion of development diplomacy.

It is also not unusual to find some government departments overplaying health pandemics for sympathetic donor support, forgetting that such publicity may also play negatively against investment opportunities. Such is life in the public service. In this regard, the importance of functional coordination cannot be over emphasized.

Local Direct Investments

Local direct investment [LDI] means local equity participation by citizens. According to [Depad. 2002] the local direct investment is the magnet that pulls foreign direct investments. The foreign capital, whatever form it may take is attracted by the movement of local capital. This is why some donors indicate that their aid money is not for charity. What they mean is the importance of shared responsibilities over development projects.

Some foreign investors are afraid to invest where citizens are not interested in equity participation. The fear is justified because national economic development is the responsibility of citizens. There is need for patriotism from all citizens in order for any national economy to develop. The absence of local investments has the implication of a hostile business environment.

Foreign investors interpret the situation in their own way. The behavior of the citizens becomes the benchmark for decisions. Therefore, it is wrong to expect much from development diplomacy when citizens have no capacity to raise partnership funds. It is the movement of local equity that provides evidence to foreigners of business opportunities available in a country. Generally the investors who are risk averse prefer to work with local partners. Partnering with the local investors provides some kind of assurances to the foreigners.

There are many forms of business partnerships. The difference is determined by the extent to which there is a dominant partner. In this regard there could be the partnership of equals, what is commonly known as the 50/50 relationship. What is important in any form of partnership is to understand the reasons for its establishment. The tactical question is on the base of hierarchical control.

Promoting Tourism

In spite of the technicalities involved, the promotion of tourism is also part of development diplomacy. This is because developing countries have recognized the importance of the industry to national economic growth. Mills [2000. p. 51] confirms that global spending on tourism more than doubled from the beginning of the 1980's; rising from US$220 billion to US$450 billion in 1997. The United States of America got the lion share of US$74.2 billion, Italy came in second with US$30.4 billion, France came in third with US$29.7 billion, Spain got US$ 29.6 billion, and the United Kingdom got US$21.3 billion, leaving the balance to other tourism destinations.

This is why hosting the Olympic Games and the World Cup has become a political issue. It is a well known fact that some developed countries have been willing to host international conferences with the objective of improving tourism revenues. Mills [2000. p. 51] reports that tourism reached a record of 625 million people traveling in 1998, nearly tripling the 260 million record high of the 1980s. He also advocates that tourism created some 255 million jobs in 1997 alone. Tourism employees include guides, baggage makers, cooks, photo shops, tour operators and telephone service providers.

Evidence exists that the visitation of one tourist to a country results in the creation of nine tourism related jobs. When discussing tourism as a potential industry, it is necessary to realize that the concept of the world as a global village has made the cost of flying cheaper. With the introduction of bigger aircrafts such as the Boeing 777 seat occupancy has become one of the strategic management issues in the airline industry. This is because empty seats cost money to the airline. During low seasons the airline industry operates on cost recovery. The same management strategy is used in the hotel industry. Mills [2000. p. 51] reports that in consequence, a round trip to Bangkok that cost an equivalent of US$10,000 in 1934 is now costing about US$600. Strangely though, the positive perception on the economic potential of tourism is at variance with existing paradigms in developing countries.

Developing countries often regard hosting of international conferences as a burden. Instead of hosting the conferences with optimism, some of them refuse by presenting flimsy excuses. Others accept to host the conferences for cheap political reasons. Instead of maximizing revenue from hotel accommodation, hotel rates for conference delegates are reduced. In some of the countries, the private sector offers accommodation subsidies to the conference delegates, including participants to international sports festivals. The subsidy is not only unwarranted but also unfair. The subsidy would be more valuable to small scale farmers for the improvement of their production capacity than to the foreigners. This is probably one of the reasons the tourism industry is still underdeveloped in these countries. It is obvious that development diplomacy will take time to become a driver of the developing economies.

Another challenge for the developing countries is that tourism is only targeted toward foreigners. The citizens in the countries are not offered incentives to visit and spend nights in local hotels, even though many of the activities the hotels offer; such as sightseeing, bird watching, fishing, hunting, the study of plants, food, transportation and many others are also attractive to the citizens.

When noteworthy personalities make reference to the importance of the tourism industry, the common message is that tourism is solely for foreigners. The attitude is wrong, from the general aim of the message, to the little things like the extra cleaning undertaken at hotels to impress the foreign guests. It is wrong because even local tourists deserve high standards of hygiene.

Consistent with such lopsided thinking, traditional cuisines enjoyed by citizens often are not served in the hotels. Among other reasons, tourists travel to experience new life and enjoy foreign food. Of what value is a holiday destination when the food available is familiar? Therefore, it is counterproductive to neglect the contributions from exotic domestic settings. It is a proven fact that tourism is a powerful driver for economic growth when planned properly. How would the economy of a country benefit from tourism when the food served to the tourists is imported? Similarly how would tourism drive the economy when hotel accommodation is offered at reduced rates during international conferences? Practical evidence suggests that the strength of any business must begin from home settings. This is how reputable businesses begin. The home setting provides the training ground for skills and competence improvements.

As demonstrated from preceding discussions, the flow of foreign direct investments follows the movement of domestic capital. When there are no domestic investments, foreign direct investments will not flow. The same principle applies to inward tourism. Even the scriptures advocate self-reliance. When domestic tourism is strong, hospitality standards also improve. And when standards improve, tourism gains an international reputation. Subsequently, it is the high standard which attracts international tourists.

Therefore, the development of local tourism also requires planning. The local tourists would also be pleased to participate in timeshare offers and packaged tours. Tourists are not rich people in their countries. They are like some of the citizens in the developing countries. They plan for a year to spend their holiday in this or that country. Citizens should also be assisted and encouraged by offering them domestic holiday packages.

When designing promotional schemes for the attraction of inward tourism, it is imperative to appreciate the influence of culture when people travel. Some cultures promote group travel and room sharing. Other cultures prefer a heavy breakfast with a wide selection of food. The tourists who travel in groups believe in sharing experiences. Group travel is impossible in the absence of luxury coaches for tourists. Therefore, some of the tourists will avoid destinations which do not have facilities for group travel. Group travelers prefer tour guides who are conversant in foreign languages. These are fundamental issues that have to be respected when contemplating the promotion of inward tourism. It is more than just offering hotel accommodations and delicious food.

Another factor influencing travel decisions by tourists is the value of services. The room rate factor is of paramount importance when selecting holiday destinations. Costs in the hotel industry should always be relative to the national economy. It is wrong to recover losses arising from poor room occupancy at the facility from the few tourists who happen to visit periodically.

Having discussed this subject at great length, the question that must be answered is how diplomatic missions would promote tourism. It is imperative to remind hotel operators that marketing requires product knowledge. It is absolutely impossible for development diplomacy to succeed when the diplomatic staffs are ignorant of quality of services in the hotels. Hotel services are intangible products which can only be appreciated when enjoyed. The hotel industry has to offer complimentary accommodation to diplomatic staffs on posting, including their spouses, so they may sample, and hopefully attest, to the services.

This is the dichotomy developing countries must resolve before expecting too much from development diplomacy. Its introduction should not be perceived as a panacea. There is a lot to be implemented before the realization of the desired results. It is not simply a matter of adopting an ideology.

It has now become apparent that the availability of strategic resources, large markets and professional skills including local investment capital are the main factors conducive to the flow of foreign direct investments. It is important to be aware of the changing investment conditions throughout the international community. The world economic outlook is no longer favorable to poor developing countries. Diplomatic missions do not operate with magic wands for them to turn impossibilities to possibilities. Foreign direct investment is on the run as different countries, including developed countries, are offering different incentives in the hope of attracting it.

Following Up Pledges

The practice of extending Official Development Assistance to poor countries is not a new phenomenon; it dates back to historic times. Usually economic aid includes technical assistance. Whatever forms the cooperation assistance may take; the fact is that it is an important component for the development of poor countries. Some of the rich developed countries report of having benefited from similar economic assistance in the past. When used wisely, economic assistance can help to speed up economic transformation of a country. The only disadvantage is that such economic assistance can act as opium to others. It is hard to cope without it in the absence of bold and proactive steps.

Oftentimes, some of the countries relying on aid are described as failed states; an insensitive remark intended to denigrate those relying on it. The remarks are not strange to believers who read the scriptures. The scriptures discourage the habit of receiving handouts. Handouts make some of the beneficiaries lazy and less creative. Regardless of the different perception on handouts, however, it has always been the responsibility of diplomatic missions to follow up aid pledges.

The key issue is not who to blame for the aid syndrome. In fact, some aid receiving countries are desperately seeking ways to escape from the poverty trap. Others are investing in agricultural production to export primary products to international commodity markets. Unfortunately, exporting the primary products is unprofitable owing to market distortions created by policies of developed countries. It has to be acknowledged that the markets are controlled by human beings. There are also producers of similar commodities in the developed countries. Naturally, the commodity merchants have a moral responsibility to offer better prices to their fellow citizens with the imports treated as top-up stocks. It is normal for the commodity traders to operate that way. The same situation would apply if the markets were controlled by the developing countries.

In this regard, the receipt of Official Development Assistance may not be easy to stop. The challenge is how to overcome underdevelopment without the technical and economic assistance from the rich developed countries when world commodity prices continue to deteriorate. Indeed, the Official Development Assistance helps the eradication of social poverty through the provision of classrooms, hospitals, medical equipment, medicines, bridges, clean water and telecommunications. However, without market access and investments, aid alone is unhelpful.

Evidence exists that some of the developing countries are making efforts to diversify their economies. They also have plans to reduce dependency on donors. What is required from the cooperating partners is a smart combination of the economic assistance with trade and investments. The developing countries need grants to undertake integrated economic development studies for new investment projects. It is obvious that foreign investors even with the best goodwill in the world cannot guess the availability of viable projects in a country when there are no feasibility studies. The feasibility studies cost money as consultants operate on international remuneration rates.

The case has already been made on the prevailing attitude of foreign investors. Their strategy is to look for partners from the local people. Without the local partners, the foreign investors would not be prepared to take risks. While diplomatic missions have the traditional responsibility to follow up aid pledges, it is clear that Official Development Assistance alone cannot overcome poverty. This view is supported by the fact that economic assistance is now targeted to pro-poor sectors, with emphasis on education and health. Obviously, the eradication of poverty requires a combination of initiatives including trade and investments.

REFERENCES:

Mills, G.[2000] – The Wired Model - South Africa,
Foreign Policy and Globalization.
1st Edn, Cape Town,
The South African Institute of International
Affairs and Tafelberg Publishers Limited.

Warren. R [2002] – The Purpose Driven Life,
Philippine Campus Crusade Edition
Purpose Driven Ministries,
Quezon City 1103.

DAPAD [2002] – INSOWEL Development Program
The DAPAD Foundation, Tokyo, Japan

CHAPTER SEVEN:

DIPLOMACY OF PARTNERSHIP – THE JAPANESE INITIATIVE

Almost all civilized countries have diplomatic relations amongst themselves. Their diplomatic relations manifest the existence of friendship. As discussed in earlier chapters, diplomatic relations mainly exists on either a bilateral or multilateral basis. Generally such relations are for the pursuance of a diversity of strategic interests. Most importantly, diplomatic relations operate on principles of mutual respect, recognition of the equality of states and national sovereignty. In spite of the existence of these international values, it is for far too long that developing countries in Africa have been on the receiving end of everything.

It is a paradox that in spite of its abundant natural resources, the African continent has the largest number of poor countries in the world. Obviously something is wrong, because God did not create poor countries. This is because countries without the resources found in Africa are rich. It is a pertinent point for Africans to understand. However, there is need to answers some questions. Why should the African continent be associated with diseases, poverty, illiteracy, wars and corruption?

A chronological study on the causes of Africa's continued underdevelopment is instructive. However, those who place their faith in Jesus Christ know that God does not hate the African people. There are people who prefer distorting the truth by associating black skin with sin. Such distortions are the work of non-believers. Believers in Christ know that skin color has nothing to do with one's relationship with God.

It is obvious that the causes of poverty in Africa are man-made. To comprehend the predicament the African people are facing, it is imperative to study the consequences of colonialism and the Cold War. One of the conceivable humiliating consequences of colonialism was its debilitating effects to cultural paradigms of the African people.

The educational system introduced by the colonizing powers was designed to achieve cultural paradigm shifts in order to create space for the inculcation of civilization. It is a well known fact that civilization was aimed at replacing the African primitive beliefs with a new culture; the problem was not civilization itself but the process used to enforce it. The process was crude and resulted in removing the self-respect and creativity of the majority of the African people. Those who resisted inculcation of the civilization were perceived as rejects, and their treatment adversely affected the thinking and attitude of some African communities.

In the colonization days, the newly civilized scandalized their neighbors as backward, and strangely, that remains the prevailing attitude in many parts of Africa today. These traits, along with the enslavement and trade of many Africans among one another, constitute the history and dehumanization of inhabitants of the African continent. What is happening in Africa today is a cause and effect of history. To reverse the situation, there is need for continued economic support for an education system that incorporates cultural studies and the teaching of the scriptures.

———————————

To say that the African people have been insensitive to their despicable situation is an understatement intended solely to denigrate them. After attaining political independence, most of the developing countries in Africa intensified efforts to promote active diplomatic relations with the international community by subscribing to the membership of almost all multilateral institutions. However, in spite of their efforts, very little was gained in terms of influence over those international issues that continued to adversely affect them.

Leaders from independent African countries attended international conferences one after another, listening to lectures on economics and politics much the way students do today. When given time to speak, it was time to pay glowing tribute to hospitality. Naturally, the events turned into speech contests with one African leader making every effort to outshine the other by the use of flowery English and political buzzwords.

While this melodramatic episode was taking place, the situation in Africa was changing from bad to worse. With the demise of the Cold War in 1991, African countries fast became economic quagmires, especially those countries which had subscribed to the eastern ideology of the Soviet Union. With many African nations betrayed by the USSR and others feeling abandoned by the international community at large, it was the government of Japan which selflessly initiated the diplomacy of partnership popularly known as the Tokyo International Conference on African Development (TICAD) in 1993.

The word "partnership" has been popularized in the private sector as it pertains to the control of market positions. In practice, the motivation for pursuing partnership schemes in the private sector could either be to defend against or catch up to the competition.

Market leaders pursue partnerships to defend against new businesses or competitors, while market followers opt for partnerships to catch up with market leaders. In regards to TICAD, the partnership scheme initiated by Japan with the developing countries in Africa was based on perceived compatibilities, capabilities and commitment towards the eradication of African poverty, with Japan and the international community acting as cooperating partners.

Ecclesiastes 4:9-12 explains this type of partnership when it states that two are better than one, because they have good return for their work. Unlike other developed nations, the Japanese people are very considerate when it comes to humanitarian assistance. Some may disagree and view this as personal opinion, but it is accurate to say that one only understands the Japanese people after visiting Japan. Print media portrayals are not always reflective of Japan and its people.

Indeed, Japan and its people are unique in themselves. One distinctive feature that differentiates the Japanese people from other nations is their experience with poverty, and the Japanese are not shy about sharing with visitors this history. The Japanese people know what it is to be poor, and they also know how to overcome poverty. This is a very important point because poverty is a generic term; it has different meanings influenced by the background of the person complaining about it.

Some people consider themselves poor because they have no food; others because they do not have good drinking water. Some associate poverty with an inability to send their children to school. All these examples are poverty profiles, but the problem is they are all subjective experiences. Unless such experiences are shared with others in similar situations, such profiles can only be treated as another story.

This is where the TICAD process becomes a meaningful complementary tool for the successful implementation of development diplomacy, the theme of this book. The TICAD process operates on the principles of partnership, ownership and cooperation.

It is a proven fact that the successful eradication of poverty cannot be achieved without involving those affected by it. For example, only those people who have had to sleep on empty stomachs can fully appreciate the plight that entails. Therefore, it is wise to involve those who have personally experienced poverty to be part of the solutions. Outsiders should only add value to the process by providing complementary economic support as cooperating partners.

The government of Japan, having once suffered poverty itself, was uniquely aware of the need for direct involvement of African leaders in the process. Japan also realized that there could not be any meaningful partnership without mutual respect and understanding. Consequently, since its inception in 1993, the TICAD process has become the strategic place for African leaders to discuss important development issues.

During the conferences, African leaders collectively share their experiences on development challenges and choose priorities on equal terms. Unlike other multilateral conferences, the process transforms the African leaders to become masters of their own destiny. The government of Japan and the international community in attendance participate as cooperating partners, not supervisors. It is noteworthy that those African leaders who attended the Third TICAD Summit in 2003 issued the 10th Anniversary Declaration in which they observed the launch of the initiative in 1993 which managed to reverse the loss of interest in Africa by the international community.

It is a challenge for the new African leaders and the government of Japan to take responsibility for the underdevelopment of African countries involving situations originally beyond their control. Just as Africa never chose to be colonized, it found itself taking sides on differing political ideologies during the Cold War, even though the consequences meant nothing to the overwhelming majority of Africans. When the war of ideology ended, the African countries were to be discarded like a peanut shell after its nuts are eaten. The African countries continued to lose despite the fact that large volumes of natural resources from the continent were plundered through unfettered exploitative schemes during the colonial and Cold War periods.

It was the introduction of the TICAD initiative by Japan that restored hope among African leaders for the development of their continent. It was in full appreciation of the importance of the development strategy that the delegates to the first TICAD conference in 1993 overwhelmingly endorsed and adopted the principles of the process. This was an endorsement aimed at achieving synergy and mutual reinforcements to the United Nations' initiatives for the Development of Africa. (For more information, read the United Nations New Agenda for the Development of Africa (UN-NADAF) in the 1990s.

This conference proved that African leaders recognized the importance of collective efforts toward development projects. It also made sense that the first conference identified the need for the establishment of shared values. In spite of ethnic diversity in Africa, African leaders present at the time identified democracy, governance and the rule of law as a few of those shared values. It was correct for the African leaders to choose democracy as a basis of cooperation as there could be no consensus without common values.

Like any good intention, the launch of the initiative by the government of Japan has not been without constraints. As if to conspire with the prophets of doom, the launch of the TICAD process coincided with a severe economic downturn in Japan. However, in spite of the economic difficulties the Japanese faced, they did not shy away from their commitment toward African development. In fact, the development of Africa remained a high priority on Japan's international agenda, and through the influence of the government of Japan, some African leaders attend the sidelines of the Group of Eight Summits. This is a great achievement for developing African countries, helping them to realize that the longest journey begins with a single step. The decision to invite the African leaders to the fringes of the Group of Eight Summits demonstrates that the TICAD process was initiated from the heart, and not for superficial reasons. At every consecutive conference since the launch of the TICAD process, the government of Japan has not failed to announce new pledges of economic assistance to African countries.

The government of Japan is committed to ensuring that the TICAD process does not become just another forum for the

Africans to meet new friends. Apart from hosting the periodic summits, Japan maintains regular contact with the African leaders by, among other things, sending senior bureaucrats and politicians on short visits to almost all the African states for the purpose of exchanging ideas while observing the actual situation on the ground. As a country that also wrestled with poverty, Japan is keenly aware of the difference between conference discussions and implementation of resolutions; between talking and taking action. These are two separate mutually reinforcing strategic events. Therefore, the launch of the 1993 TICAD process was followed by the organization of two operational regional workshops in Africa. One regional meeting was held in Zimbabwe in 1996, followed by a second one in Côte d'Ivoire. The regional meetings were held after the first Asia Africa Forum (AAFI) hosted by Indonesia in 1994. The Asia Africa Forum is yet another strategic approach by the government of Japan aimed at mobilizing regional support from the countries of Southeast Asia, in the form of collective approach towards African development. The government of Japan hosted the first ever TICAD - Asia Africa Trade and Investment Conference involving senior government officials together with captains of industry in November, 2004. The purpose of the TICAD Asia-Africa Trade and Investment Conference (AATIC) is to help African countries realize sustainable and self-reliant economic growth by applying vigor of the private sector as well as ODA by the public sector, which would contribute to reducing poverty and achieving international development agendas including the Millennium Development Goals (MDGs).

Once again the importance of synergy and collective responsibility is evident in Japan's involvement with the African continent. This helps to explain why the TICAD conferences have always been co-organized by Japan, the United Nations' Office of the Special Coordinator for Africa and the Least Developed Countries (OSCAL). Note: *this office was recently renamed as Office of Special Assistant for Africa – OSAA.*

From TICAD II, UNDP and the Global Coalition for Africa became co-organizers, proving that Japan does not act unilaterally in international relations. The World Bank is also one of the co-organizers since TICAD II. Notwithstanding that a decade has elapsed since the first TICAD conference, there are others who fail to appreciate the importance of the principle of mutual reinforcements. Instead of joining forces for the African leaders not to waste time on attending meetings, some in the international community are in the business of creating new initiatives all the time. This is sad because the TICAD process has overcome its teething problems; it now has a 10-year knowledge base and a solid foundation for continued success. The involvement of Southeast Asia countries in the TICAD process also demonstrates the intrinsic value the government of Japan places on collective effort. It makes sense for Japan to involve its regional neighbors in the process. The impressive and rapid economic transformation of the Southeast Asian region serve as a living testimony of how poor countries can change course and build toward prosperity. And it proves that with commitment and hard work, the developing countries of Africa can also transform their economies.

The development of the Southeast Asian countries helps to demonstrate that poverty is not a permanent condition for specific ethnic groups. As discussed at the beginning of this chapter, the color of one's skin has no meaning to God. All human beings are equal before God. First and foremost, economic transformation requires placing faith in God by believing in the teachings of our Lord Jesus Christ. Thereafter, there is need for the spirit of improvement and betterment based upon those resources and blessings God purposely provided in the country. When citizens of a country are determined and realize the comparative advantages given to them by God, there is nothing to stop or hinder their country from development.

Most Asian countries were just as poor as many of the African countries. Now they are enjoying great economic growth through the resolve and determination of their citizens. It is from this remarkable achievement that the Japanese government can show its commitment to helping others. Japan differs from other developed countries in that it has real examples of countries it has helped develop to economic prosperity.

Indeed, the government of Japan deserves commendation for assisting the countries of Southeast Asia to transform their economies to the success they now enjoy. As part of the TICAD process, the aim of the 1994 Asia-Africa Forum (AAFI) was to promote direct dialogue and an exchange of ideas between African and Asian policymakers. It was the expectation that through consultations at the forum, a consensus would emerge on specific Asian policy experiences that could benefit Africa. The desired objectives for the forum were achieved as demonstrated by the adoption of the Bandung Framework for Asia African Cooperation. Truthfully, no country can develop without learning from others.

This was the same way Emperor Meiji developed Japan from 1868 to 1912. Inukai [2003. p.1] explains that the first decade (1868 to 1877) was a period of initial problems when necessary conditions had to be created for economic growth. The second decade (1878 to 1887) was the period for the training of public servants, and establishing the economic and administrative infrastructure. The third decade (1888 to 1897) was the period for economic growth. At the core of the growth period was the human factor. Training was the major ingredient of the young Emperor's development plans. Historical nuggets of information like this provide lessons to the developing countries in Africa through exchange of ideas at the TICAD Asia-Africa Forum.

Every time the TICAD conference is hosted, Tokyo becomes an African village. The African leaders are accompanied by their spouses and bureaucrats who are backed by their diplomatic representatives whom reside in Tokyo. The Third Tokyo International Conference on African Development was organized from September 29th to October 1st 2003 in Tokyo. The city of Tokyo indeed transformed into an African village with twenty-three African Heads of State or Government in attendance. When Japanese Prime Minister Junichiro Koizumi presided over the official opening of the conference, he couldn't help but notice the presence of so many African leaders. In fact, Prime Minister Koizumi was pleased to describe the city of Tokyo as an African village. It further pleased him to qualify and quantify the commitment the government of Japan has to the TICAD process by specifically referencing the economic assistance extended to the African countries since the inception of the TICAD process in 1993.

The Japanese Prime Minister was pleased to assure his distinguished guests that the Government of Japan was tackling African development issues with tangible actions, not just words. He announced that since the inception of the process in the last decade, the government of Japan had implemented assistance programs amounting to US $12 billion to African countries. He also informed his distinguished guests that the government of Japan had trained more than 10,000 Africans in capacity building during the same period. Prime Minister Koizumi expressed happiness when noting that over 7000 Japanese experts were serving in African countries at the time of the conference. Considering that many believe that underdevelopment is a security threat, the number of Japanese experts in Africa illustrates that the government and people of Japan are indeed committed to helping African countries to develop.

Speaking at the same conference in his capacity as the chairperson of the 2003 conference, and also as the first Japanese incumbent Prime Minister to have visited Africa, former Prime Minister Yoshiro Mori reiterated his conviction that worldwide stability and prosperity in the 21st century would be impossible unless the problems facing Africa were resolved. The former Prime Minister's support suggests that he is Japanese with an African heart. Currently, the former Prime Minister is the chairperson of the African Union Parliamentary Friendship League; the League that was established to further deepen relations with Africa.

These conferences and events are part of the TICAD initiatives which will result in more media coverage of African visits. There is a popular adage in Asia that says, *"the longest journey begins with a single step."* Certainly, what the government has done is more that a single step. The effort has been continuous and incremental. Many Africans proudly call former Prime Minister Yoshiro Mori the true friend of Africa.

What is exceptional about the partnership initiated by the government of Japan is that it was based on a heart to heart relationship. It is not a calculated relationship like that practiced by the private sector which often translates into gaining market advantages. On the contrary, the economic and technical assistance offered by the government of Japan to Africa has no strings attached. Japanese economic assistance is extended to African countries without counting the number of times such assistance is provided; it is based on verified needs by the communities. In this regard, the Africans need to work together to derive the maximum benefits from the strategic and generous process initiated by the government of Japan. It is not the government of Japan that must lead; the African governments must lead while Japan follows.

An effective partnership requires all the stakeholders to play their roles. The outcome with the TICAD process so far has been quite positive. Gradually, some African countries are improving their economies, and slowly Africa has been regaining stature from the international community. The only problem remaining is that some in the international community continue to view Africa as a burden. Consequently, the treatment by these countries is calculative.

In this regard, all efforts should be taken by Africans themselves to identify the government of Japan and its citizens as true partners. It would be sad to forget that the strategic posture gained with TICAD is not the natural order of things. Without the timely intervention by the government of Japan, the current situation in Africa might have been worse. No effort must be spared to refrain losing that which has already been gained. This is a relationship marketing exercise that rests on genuine friendship and the common good.

Program Partnership

Following the 9/11 terrorist attacks on the United States of America in New York City, the world's geopolitical situation took a dramatic turn. Since 9/11 the international community has been preoccupied by the war against terrorism. Once again, as was previously the case, the international community's glowing interest in the African countries has begun to fade. In spite of its commitment to Africa, Japan's responsibility as the second largest economy in the world forces it to participate in other international roles. In this regard the importance of the Asia/Africa cooperation cannot be overemphasized. On the strength of this transcontinental alliance, it is important for Africa to harmonize its development needs through institutional initiatives.

This also requires demonstrating how fiscal harmonization without market harmonization would facilitate the realization of overall development. The process of integration should not be selective. Africa needs a better understanding of itself when it comes to imports and exports. Why should it be cheaper to trade with countries outside the continent when the products are readily available across the border? In some cases it could be cheaper to import some agricultural commodities from across the border than maintaining those routes sustained since the colonial economic constitution. Some African countries import coffee from outside the continent when Africa is the major producer of Arabica coffee. The list of the commodities is long; it suffices to suggest that the TICAD process should also help to introduce a new way of thinking within Africa.

Consistent with the spirit of partnership and ownership, African leaders deserve commendation for establishing the New Partnership for Africa's Development (NEPAD) as a program for promoting development diplomacy with the international community. Through the offices of the New Partnership for Africa's Development, African countries should be able to present a basket of regionally integrated development projects to cooperating partners. In spite of the multilateral character of the TICAD process, the government of Japan also uses it as an apparatus for the delivery of bilateral programs; it is necessary that a balancing act is maintained to ensure that bilateral development projects are not overshadowed by the pursuit of multilateralism. There cannot be regional prosperity without country specific prosperity. Individual countries need feeder roads and bridges in order to make regional road projects viable. Countries need elementary and high schools in order to have sufficient students for regionally based tertiary institutions. At a glance this may create the impression of serious contradictions, but in reality it is mutually reinforcing.

This is where the TICAD process emerges as the only multilateral institution with a human face. Its processes are governed by consensus on priority projects. The process distinguishes itself from others in that it provides a convenient place for the African leaders to plan together their development priorities without prescriptions. Like the operations of any other strategic institution, there is no way resource requirement and resource availability can be equal; there will be occasions when the resource pendulum will fail.

However, the advantage is that the process has provision for interim monitoring through various intercessional meetings. The meetings attended by cabinet ministers from within the African governments are aimed at reviewing progress before the next TICAD summit. The fourth TICAD conference will be hosted by the government of Japan in 2008. There is optimism that by that time, the status of development in many African countries will have changed for the better.

Before closing the discussions on the role played by the TICAD process in uplifting the international image and the economic transformation of Africa, it is fair to give the government of Japan the credit for initiating the concept of development diplomacy in 1993. This is because the TICAD process recognizes the importance of a smart partnership between government and the private sector. Development diplomacy means the interaction between the two sectors. The government of Japan hosted the TICAD ASIA-AFRICA Trade and Investment Conference from 1st-2nd November in 2004 which was the practice of development diplomacy. Obviously the conference will mark a strategic new step for change from dependency on aid to market access and the flow of foreign direct investments. It has been proven that aid alone without improved market access and the flow of foreign direct investment cannot result in the economic development of any poor country. The problem with economic assistance is that it is often targeted at eradicating social poverty. Social investments have long term effects on the economy, making the consolidation of democracy an impossible task.

As always, there is a tendency of taking the success of conferences for granted. Success requires planning and leadership. There is palpable evidence that before hosting the TICAD III Conference in 2003, a lot of hard work was done behind the scenes. The Director-General for Sub-Saharan Africa, Ambassador Masaharu Kohno spent sleepless nights coordinating and planning for the conference. Senator Tetsuro Yano who was then Senior Vice Minister for Foreign Affairs undertook a number of visits to Africa to brief African leaders on the conference. Members of the African diplomatic corps resident in Tokyo also worked hard on logistics and protocol arrangements. The success of the TICAD III conference was therefore the culmination of many positive efforts.

John Chikago

<u>REFERENCES:</u>

Inukai .I [2003] – Japan's First Strategy for Economic
Development, Copyright Edition,
International Development Program Press
Niigata, Japan.

ACT 2003 (TICADIII) – Collection of Statements and
Proposals of the International
Conferences Relative to Africa
Development 1993-2003

CHAPTER EIGHT:

TIME MANAGEMENT

According to Genesis 1:3-5; time was created when God declared there should be day and night at the dawn of creation. The assumption that time is a scientific discovery is not only wrong but also unbiblical. The watch is an invention made possible by man-made scientific discovery. People traveling the globe understand the meaning of time. When nightfall descends in one country, another country is enjoying daylight. In that way there is no moment when all people in the world are sleeping. Consequently, it is sometimes difficult to communicate with friends across the globe before reviewing the different time zones. God is wonderful indeed.

The problem of time is that it is elusive. Time is not easy to manage. Usually the value of time is only appreciated after it is lost. This is one of the reasons many people complain about having lost time here or there. The major problem with time is on its application as sometimes it is misunderstood as a status symbol; whereby senior managers are expected to report at work late; relaxation time for shop floor workers is idle time. In some communities it is not unusual for scheduled meetings to start late in order to wait for the chairperson. Naturally, the waiting time is not associated with loss of opportunities.

Obviously, God was aware of the need for His living creatures to rest; resting through sleep was God's plan. After sleeping, lost energy is restored. Surprisingly, there are some people in developing countries who do not realize that God has given mankind day and night for a purpose. Such people spend the night sleeping. When they wake in the morning, they have no plans for their day; instead they spend the whole day loitering around without doing anything productive.

The tendency is contrary to the word of God in Genesis 3: 19. The message from the scriptures is clear; people have to live on their sweat. Therefore, it is against God's will for anyone to live unproductive life. Except for the sick and frail, food must be taken after working hard. By allocating the same period of time for day and night, God wanted His people to work at least as much as they rested. It should not surprise believers to learn that poverty remains problematic in the world. No one anywhere in the world can prosper without understanding and putting into practice what the word of God says.

Time has been associated with many meanings by the business community. The business community measures time in seconds, minutes, hours, half days, days, weeks, months, seasons and years with the objective of maximizing profits. The fact that time has different measurements in the private sector shows that it is a valuable resource. It is only when everyone gains this insight that the management of time will be taken seriously. The business community recognizes the importance of time to business performance. It is aware of the exceptional importance globalization has given to time-based competition. Instead of gaining market leadership through quality and price, delivery time has become the main factor. Now it is the response time to customer orders that matters. Customers cannot wait indefinitely for cheap products nor wait for a long time to buy quality products. Consequently, when customers look for prices and quality they also want to know the delivery time for the product. Considering that development diplomacy is an interface between the private and public sectors, it is advisable to establish shared values on the meaning of time.

In chemistry there is a simple principle that says *the like will dissolve the like*. Oil cannot dissolve in water. It is from this fundamental principle, among other things, that the public sector should be subjected to dramatic cultural paradigm shifts.

It is common knowledge that the private sector treats time with exceptional interests. The value given to time can be explained by the influx of descriptive terminologies such as, time on tasks, deadlines, guaranteed delivery dates, lead time and cycle time. All these terms give monetary value to time. To the contrary, the perception is different in the public sector. The public sector treats time as a valueless resource which is always in plentiful supply. These are serious and divergent values to the same thing. Unless the different cultural perceptions are narrowed down, diplomatic staff will have a hard-selling job in their hands.

The proof that the private sector looks at time as money derives from the practice of keeping time records. These records are used as a basis for monitoring production efficiency, product costing, capacity planning, payment of bonuses and input data for the calculation of productivity levels. Some manufacturing companies have specific cost and management accounting departments which are mandated to monitor the usage of time. An army of time clerks is deployed to record production time. These records also provide information when calculating resource capacity utilization.

As pointed out elsewhere, the public sector, on the other hand, does not treat time as a management tool. Time is only related to lunch break and closing time in the afternoon. In both cases, it is a matter of serving the personal interests of employees. The value of time is only known to the public sector when making overtime payments; owing to negative budgetary implications.

The success of development diplomacy requires an immediate cultural paradigm shift. The public sector must accord the same value and importance to time as is the case in the private sector. It is not a matter of choice but of necessity. The success of the private sector is based on efficient management of time. Arrival at the work place is on time. Meetings are conducted on time; the meetings are arranged to ensure equitable distribution of human resources. The effective management of time enables one manager to attend two or more meetings in one day. It is a matter of achieving more with fewer resources. Unless diplomatic staffs are acquainted with that culture, it will be difficult to achieve an effective interface with the private sector.

Time Based Competition

It has been pointed out that among other things; modern competition is based on time. Therefore, businesses all over the world have to efficiently manage the usage of time in order to remain competitive. In the absence of time management, prices of products and services would become expensive. Production planning and control would not be easy. Consequently, it would not be possible to decide on the number of workers to employ. Apart from the need to control operational costs, the knowledge of time is important for improving service delivery. Poor service delivery is a recipe for customer dissatisfaction and loss of loyalty.

There are some customers who are willing to pay higher prices for fast services. In recent years it has become fashionable for young men to buy highly priced, powerful sports cars. In Japan, many commuters prefer to travel long distances on high speed trains commonly known as *Shinkasen*. When choosing the high speed trains the commuters take full cognizance of cost implications. The commuters do not care paying more for the high speed trains. They are prepared to spend more than waste time on riding ordinary trains which are slower. In this way the *Shinkasen* has gained high popularity among commuters for speed.

Another point to be appreciated when advocating the pursuance of development diplomacy is the importance of supply lead times to commodity importers. Long supply lead times cause businesses to carry high stocks. The maintenance of high stock levels in a business binds working capital. This is why some businesses prefer using materials which are available locally. Using local material has two advantages: it is available when needed. Financial resources are not tied up in the stocks. This is what makes the Toyota Motor Corporation a highly competitive automobile company in the world.

Most of the outsourced parts at the Toyota Factory in Nagoya are supplied by small companies located within the factory's neighborhood. The parts are only ordered on the basis of a material requirement plan for immediate production. This type of stock control is commonly known as *just in time*. The usage of the word *time* reflects its strategic importance to the assembly line. It is therefore necessary to appreciate the positive effects of supply lead times when promoting commodity exports. Importers have to be assured of supply lead times because some products have seasonal demands. Suppose a retailer in Japan is interested to import woolen material from a source that has a supply lead time of six months. When would the order be placed and whose capital would be tied-up during that period?

Some investors dislike dealing with people who take time to make decisions. The investors associate the slow decision making to corruption. Naturally, the investors take other market options, owing to the existence of other equally attractive investment destinations. In this instance, how would development diplomacy facilitate quick decision making back at home? Unless the systems management approach discussed in earlier chapters is adopted in the holistic sense; the diplomatic missions should not be blamed for failing to attract foreign direct investments.

The other sector in which time management is important is the hospitality industry. Slow services disappoint customers. As indicated elsewhere modern tourists prefer group travel, and when group members complain about service delays, the affected group will leave the destination with negative feelings. The whole group is disappointed. This is one disadvantage of tourists who travel in groups. Nevertheless, group travel has become fashionable in recent years because of discount air tickets. Another point to remember is that modern tourists have interest in seeing as many places as possible during a short holiday; one reason why such tourists prefer circuit routes with a number of flight interconnections. Flight interconnections require sufficient time for transit arrangements, and failure to travel on time means missing flight connections.

The foregoing synopsis only helps to demonstrate the importance of efficient time management to development diplomacy. It is necessary for those advocating the change to development diplomacy to have this picture in mind. The implementation of development diplomacy will become a pipedream if the public sector will not change the existing attitude towards time. Time management should not be a choice but a way of life. The private sector knows and understands this; it is one of its secret success factors. The staffs at diplomatic missions have to share these values otherwise no harmonious relationship will emerge between the two sectors. Time has become the driving force for competition; even countries are now being rated on how long it takes them to make decisions. Time inevitably creates lasting impressions.

———————————

The need for responsibility and accountability to correspond has also been discussed in previous chapters. Development diplomacy is bound to fail if the bases for the two functions will be separated. It would be unfair for the staff at the diplomatic missions to account for lack of investments when the responsibility for performance is elsewhere. The introduction of development diplomacy means the line ministries responsible for the management of diplomatic missions should have the power to expedite decision making.

Wastage of Time

Many people complain about telephones, meetings and visitors as some of the time wasters at diplomatic missions. Unfortunately, the visitors, meetings and telephones are part of development diplomacy. Like anything else, there is nothing that can be achieved without planning for them. However, not all meetings are important. There has to be some kind of classification system to assess the importance of meetings. Similarly, not all visitors are important at the diplomatic mission. There are some who should be met at convenient places such as the coffee shops and residences. On the issue of telephones, it is advisable not to give out personal telephone numbers to everyone in order to avoid direct contacts. There should be a system of classifying incoming telephones to minimize disturbances.

The need to manage time effectively cannot be overemphasized regarding the number of holidays observed at diplomatic missions. Diplomatic missions are the first culprits when it comes to wastage of time. Among other things, the diplomatic missions observe too many public holidays.

A normal year has 365 days. Out of the days, there are Sundays and Saturdays. According to international practice, almost every country observes national public holidays. However, the number of national holidays varies from country to country.

In conformity with established diplomatic practice; diplomatic staffs are also expected to observe holidays in the country of assignment. In this regard, the staffs at the diplomatic missions observe a high number of national public holidays in a year. When added to annual holidays based on entitlements, it means some of the staffs at diplomatic missions spend a disproportionate amount of time on holidays. Obviously, the policies on holidays need to be reviewed to enhance the interaction between the private and public sectors. Business people know that holidays by implication cost money. As a cost reduction measure they only observe few of them.

With the poor time management culture, it is clear that the promotion of development diplomacy will be a difficult task. How would investors, traders and tourists meet with the diplomatic staff when they are on holiday most of the time? Investors are not waiting for one country. Irrespective of justification, holidays are unproductive. Holidays cost money because employees are paid for doing nothing.

Needless to say some of the holidays observed are meaningless. Do diplomatic staffs really have to observe a tree planting holiday taking place back home? Tree planting is an action; why should the country's diplomatic staff observe an action oriented holiday overseas? Likewise, some international public holidays are observed twice; different countries choose different dates for the same holiday. In the interest of development diplomacy it is advisable to exempt the diplomatic missions from some of the international public holidays on the understanding that they would be observed in the countries of assignments. Action oriented holidays should also be reviewed to make them meaningful and relevant to those living in foreign countries.

There is no doubt to believe the implementation of development diplomacy has been oversimplified. Some think that the introduction of development diplomacy is merely a matter of following fashion; it is the question of matching with others. As noted elsewhere, the term development diplomacy has been over used by bureaucrats when referring to the practice of modern diplomacy. Such a shallow approach is a recipe for failure. There is need for complete paradigm change. The change should be implemented holistically in the public sector.

Evidence has been produced to show that time management is an important competitive tool. Countries are rated as good or bad on their response time to decision making. Diplomatic missions should therefore treat time as money; indeed, time is money in kind. Its use should be subjected to the same audit procedures as money. Unfortunately, time is elusive; no one feels anything when it is being lost. Once lost, it can never be regained. It is therefore a perishable commodity. Those who have lost it when boarding an aircraft know this. Depending on traffic, it might take as much as a week before boarding the next flight.

Time is a resource that when controlled properly can offer many benefits. When time is controlled, one's life becomes peaceful; blood pressure isn't raised causing illness or worse. The work place becomes organized, creating accurate cost and pricing structures. Citizens in some developing countries are suffering from high inflation rates due to poor time management.

Fortunately, the effective use of time does not require huge investments. It all starts with planning. Imagine spending money without planning. The result is wastage. Regardless of the sum of money involved, it is advisable to prepare a budget. It is also advisable to keep a score card on the usage of time so that the day's activities are monitored in an orderly fashion. At the end of the day, it is necessary to calculate the time resource utilization ratio by dividing the time spent on doing productive work with the attendance time. When the calculations are completed, management will have better control of the work situation. It is disappointing to note that on average, the busiest worker has roughly 55% of productive time with the rest wasted on unproductive activities including relaxation allowance.

The implementation of development diplomacy should be accompanied by the introduction of productivity improvement management techniques such as time measurement and method study. Unless the management of time is changed, there will be no benefit from development diplomacy. The other constraining factor that needs change is the remuneration system in the public sector. There cannot be any improvement to time management when remuneration is not based on performance. The strange culture of rewarding poor performers even when evidence exists of bad work habits should be discouraged. The status quo is self-defeating and hopeless.

<u>REFERENCES:</u>

Bible – The New International Version

CHAPTER NINE:

STAFF APPRAISAL SYSTEMS

Staff appraisal systems are used to evaluate job performance. Torrington/Hall [1998.p 320] argues that appraisal systems have different objectives which are often in conflict. In the absence of job evaluation, the staff appraisal systems may not be the correct basis for salary reviews. Torrington/Hall [1998.p600] advises that it is necessary for salary reviews to include other factors such as market rate and equity. In that sense, the introduction of staff appraisal systems at diplomatic missions must be approached with care. The advice underlines the importance of preparing purpose statements, operating objectives and performance targets at every diplomatic mission. Nevertheless, the need to appraise staff performance is biblical. God created people with different gifts; no two people have the same gift.

The scriptures bear testimony to mankind's differences in capabilities. Matthew 25:15 tells the story of three workers who had different capabilities. The punishment for those with poor capabilities is given in verses 29-30. There is no tolerance for poor performance in the Bible. The Bible describes the worker who did not perform to expectation as useless, and fit for the darkness.

Development diplomacy as a new strategy for development requires a different approach to staff management. In the absence of clear performance standards and job evaluation systems, efforts to monitor individual contributions at diplomatic missions would become difficult. The word "monitoring" involves comparisons between standards and actual results. In life, the word monitoring is often loosely used for someone supervising work. Unless the work being supervised has clearly set standards, it is wrong to give the impression of monitoring and controlling.

Unlike in the public sector, staff appraisal systems are very popular in the private sector. This may explain why the quality of management is poor in the public sector. Without conducting staff appraisal and job evaluation systems, there is no way staff training needs can be identified. No wonder the objectionable myth of job security in the public sector irrespective of performance lives on. Some of those joining the public sector do so under the illusion of job security. Even lazy workers join the public service with the belief of job security. It would not be disrespectful to describe some of those joining the public sector directly from University as people afraid of taking challenges.

Some fear is justified regarding the way the private sector conducts staff appraisals. Generally, staff appraisals in the private sector are limited only to employees and stock movements. The main objective of such performance measurements is declaring profits for company's shareholders. When profitability is threatened, employees are the first to be punished by withholding their increments, and sometimes their annual bonus. This is because most of the staff appraisal systems are subjective, irrelevant and outdated. The state in which they are qualifies them as achieves candidates.

Considering that staff performance is a combination of many variables at the workplace such as work organization and the availability of materials, it is unfortunate that the performance appraisal systems are restricted to employees in the private sector. The practice is vulnerable to legal challenge in a court of law. The practice is not only wrong, but also a violation of human rights. It amounts to exploitation. A good starting point in understanding the unfairness of the practice can be demonstrated by the example of a professional cook employed in a kitchen without cooking utensils. The cook's employment would be in name only because there would be nothing with which to cook. Assuming the cook is impatient, it is likely the subsequent decision would be to quit. This example helps to show how institutional inadequacies impact negatively on staff performance. It is wrong to exclude institutional influences from staff performance. This explains the mutuality of staff appraisal and job evaluation systems.

The need for the public sector to appreciate the operational problem of staff appraisal systems is more relevant now than ever before. The implementation of development diplomacy has brought up the need. The change to development diplomacy should not be a matter of changing labels; nor should diplomacy be treated as the problem. It is a fundamental requirement for corresponding changes to super-ordinate goals, skills, systems, structures and staff to follow.

Therefore, the implementation of development diplomacy will require the public sector to introduce a new management culture. It is superstitious to believe that development diplomacy will succeed because everybody in the world is talking about it. There is need for many other things to change. Those interested in the change should place their faith in the teachings of the Bible. The Bible teaches that God created human beings only after everything else was created. Why didn't God create human beings first and finish with the ants and trees? This means God has an economic plan for every country. Failure to begin with God will result in the "grasshopper movement" – there will be a lot of rhetoric without any real benefit going to the people.

In other words, the status quo continues. Development diplomacy will be another terminology for those studying development economics.

The relevant question at this point would be the usefulness of implementing development diplomacy before the introduction of staff appraisal and job evaluation systems. Development diplomacy is performance related; the importance of staff appraisals to performance improvement cannot be doubted. As globalization intensifies, the economies of many developing countries will continue to worsen. The current disillusionment by citizens against the operations of diplomatic missions will further decline from desperation to hopelessness. A brother will be jealous of his own brother's achievements; a sister will feel unhappy at her sister's success. Ultimately, there will be no economic progress, only anarchism. This is the challenge development diplomacy is expected to overcome.

Although the way the private sector conducts performance measurements is not fair, there is evidence that when staff appraisals have been introduced, an increase in productivity has been observed. Practically, the introduction of staff appraisals has three advantages. First, it helps to simplify the administration of salaries; second, it provides information to management on the performance of subordinate staff which is useful for human resource planning. Finally, staff appraisals provide opportunity to identify training needs for staff development. Implemented transparently and impartially with the full cooperation of all employees, staff appraisals help to promote harmonious working relationships between management and workers. The staff appraisal systems place employees in active positions, controlling the consequence of their own actions. In other words, the employees become their own bosses.

Precondition
for Effective Staff Appraisals

The other precondition for the successful implementation of development diplomacy is staff performance. Consequently, there are divergent schools of thought on qualifications and type of staff to work at diplomatic missions. The reality is that it was not the staff who failed to perform during the Cold War period. Irrespective of the professional qualifications, the promotion of development diplomacy will depend on many other factors including the effective monitoring of staff performance. It is necessary to appreciate that performance monitoring should not be limited to the staff, but the whole public sector. The diplomatic missions do not work in isolation of other departments of government. Therefore, it is imperative to introduce inclusive, transparent and objective appraisal and job evaluation systems.

In practice, staff appraisal systems face a number of operational challenges. Some of those responsible for conducting the staff appraisal systems tend to welcome them as time-consuming exercises; others view them as irrelevant. Undoubtedly, these are some of the reasons the staff appraisal systems have been unpopular in the public sector. Public offices are unique in the way they operate; unlike private offices, they have complex social objectives arising from the fact that the main purpose of government is to address needs of citizens. Conversely, private businesses address exclusive choices by citizens through market forces, in which case staff appraisals in the public sector have to be conducted with extreme case.

There is need to observe the practical aspects distinguishing the public sector from private sector. Deductive logic may not be the basis for decision making when conducting the staff appraisals in the public service.

It's also important to remember there is always a price to any good thing. While staff appraisals assist in improving productivity in the workplace, there is also a need to ensure that they are properly implemented. Staff appraisal systems have to pass a critical test of legality. It is important to ensure that the appraisal system is consistent with the requirements of labor and human rights laws to the extent of discrimination against gender, age or sex. Barring the physically challenged should not be allowed; all employees should be treated equally. To achieve objectivity, the appraisal systems should be based on agreed standards such as the purpose statement, objectives, and targets including job descriptions. In other words, staff appraisals should not focus on personal traits nor should it be a matter of liking someone's face or voice.

In practice, an overwhelming majority of public servants lack the skills necessary to conduct an effective staff appraisal. In this case, the introduction of an effective staff appraisal system needs prior training. The diplomatic staff to conduct the staff appraisals should be trained on the need to set verifiable and achievable targets. Generally, subordinate staffs prefer their work to contain challenges. It is unreasonable to expect high performance from subordinate staff that lack capabilities and job skills. This underlines the importance of developing appropriate job descriptions against which the performance of the diplomatic staff would be evaluated.

It is imperative to ensure that the skills and experience of staff at diplomatic missions meet the challenges associated with the promotion of development diplomacy. Nothing could be achieved when the staffs lack necessary skills in the promotion of trade, tourism and investments; people give what they have, as the old English adage says, "You cannot force blood from a stone." Similarly the diplomatic staffs that lack skills and experience should not be blamed for not delivering. Rightly so, they can only give what they have in their minds.

The other requirement is the need to match performance with rate of pay. This is where information from job evaluation systems is necessary. The rate of pay has to provide incentive for more effort while taking into account market rate and equity; failure to compensate hard work demoralizes employees. According to Torrington/Hall [1998.p600] it is not advisable to pay staff only in relation to performance or contribution. Developments in the labor market have also to be considered. Obviously the needs of diplomatic staff are many; it is impossible for governments to satisfy them all at once. The most pressing needs are related to the payment of reasonable levels of living allowances, career promotions and some meritorious awards. Reinforcement of positive achievements in diplomatic service is a popular strategy in Asia.

The foregoing discussion shows that it is not merely a matter of introducing a staff appraisal system; there is also a need to reinforce achievements with incentives. Employees are motivated by positive recognition of their efforts.

What is to be Appraised?

As discussed elsewhere, the private sector uses staff appraisal systems to evaluate personal traits such as behavior and personality. That is wrong. Effective staff appraisal systems should be practical, transparent and objective. Most importantly, effective staff appraisal systems should aim at evaluating performance on the job and results achieved. At no time should the staff appraisals be misused to evaluate or judge personal traits. Focusing on personal traits will result in subjective measurements which have nothing to do with job performance.

In this regard, it is not possible to conduct an effective staff appraisal without a job description. Care must be exercised to ensure that job descriptions being used are frequently updated. They also have to be relevant. This is because over time duties for some staff change. Therefore, apart from the purpose statements, diplomatic staff should be familiar with the meaning of job descriptions. Job descriptions are helpful for appraisers to concentrate on job content and not the employee's behavior. The point is that good employees should be judged for what they contribute to the organization.

As diplomatic missions are located in different foreign countries with different comparative advantages, the appraisal systems cannot be the same. Some diplomatic stations are good sources for Official Development Assistance. Some diplomatic stations are located where there are huge tourist markets; other diplomatic stations are in places where international commodity markets are located. All these are different strategic interests requiring different approaches.

Therefore, there is a need for each diplomatic mission to be classified in relation to its strategic potential. Just as it is unfair to appraise personal traits, it is also unfair to subject the diplomatic staff to irrelevant appraisals. The guiding principle when conducting staff appraisals is to ensure that the focus is on the job. Past and present performances have to be evaluated, not some imaginary future predictions. There is a dangerous paradigm of treating staff appraisals as a one-time annual exercise. That tendency should not be condoned. Fair staff appraisals should be conducted on a day-to-day basis and continuously for the whole year. The annual event should be a mere formality. Some staff appraisals are instituted when something has gone wrong with the aim of punishing culprits. That practice is also counterproductive. God wants honesty when dealing with one another.

Choice of Staff Appraisal System

When choosing the type of staff appraisal system, it is advisable to avoid those with subjective measurements. A good staff appraisal system should meet the criteria of objectivity, practicality, and transparency, thus ensuring that the appraisal process is acceptable by all staff at the diplomatic mission. While staff appraisal systems are required to comply with legislative imperatives, there is no legislation that recommends a specific appraisal system. The choice is subjective in order to ensure relevance to the culture of the organization.

In this regard, the appraisal system should not be a transplant or copycat from other organizations. The appraisal system cannot be effective when merely copied from another organization. An appraisal method that works well in the private sector has no guarantee that it will also work well in the public sector. Similarly, an appraisal method that worked well in a certain developing country has no guarantee of succeeding elsewhere. A good staff appraisal system must be developed from within the organization; it must be informed by the culture of the organization. Like any good thing, the appraisal technique has to be reviewed from time to time to make sure of its practicality and legality.

The private sector has used many different types of staff appraisal systems; however, almost all focus on personal traits and subjectivity. This is a major weakness which should not be inherited by the public sector. The best candidate system must pass the test of relevance, transparency and objectivity. Most of the staff appraisal systems suffer from the human weaknesses of halo effect and central tendency. Consequently, some appraisers choose to play it safe by taking the middle way, thus avoiding hurting anyone. Sometimes it is a matter of who one knows. While effort must be taken to avoid favoritism, there is no staff appraisal system that is foolproof. Some staff appraisal systems lack consistency; the same system when used in another government department may yield different results.

It is generally accepted that staff appraisal systems suffer from human weaknesses caused by appraisers. A good analogy might be a gun. No gun is dangerous in itself unless used wrongly. This is why some people plead for clemency after committing homicide with the gun. Similarly, staff appraisal methods suffer from human weakness caused by prejudices, although some rating errors are committed subconsciously. Appraisal errors caused subconsciously relate to central tendency, first impressions and "like me" judgments. The like me judgment can be influenced by many things, such as originating from the same home district, having attended the same school, and having similar past experiences. Such tendencies have devastating consequences to staff morale with some losing confidence in the appraisal systems.

The foregoing discussions demonstrate that it is not easy to implement staff appraisal systems in the public service. It should be obvious that the change to development diplomacy is not an end in itself, but a means to an end. There is a lot to be done in order to derive benefits from its implementation. Senior diplomatic staffs have to be trained on how to conduct fair and effective appraisals on their subordinates. In turn, the subordinates have to be trained to accept results of the appraisals as a basis for training and career development. This underlines the importance of using time and patience in management. The benefits from the change to development diplomacy will take many years to be realized. What is required is determination and faith in God. God does not bless sinful initiatives in which human beings are treated as objects.

Conducting the Appraisal

The question concerning who should conduct the appraisal begs another one – who should be subjected to the appraisal? Traditionally, appraisal systems were designed to assess the performance of subordinate employees. However, the need to harmonize employment practices necessitated the extension of the appraisal systems to other grades of employees including senior staff. Therefore, the appraisal should be conducted by the immediate supervisor to the subordinate being appraised. To have merit, it must be conducted in an open and transparent manner. The appraiser must have firsthand knowledge of the employee and the job that is involved. This requirement reinforces the importance of making staff appraisals a day-to-day exercise.

The feasibility of appraisal systems in the public service will become problematic. There is a tendency in the public service of entrusting the responsibility of staff appraisals to bureaucrats who have no practical experience from any diplomatic mission. What value can such inexperienced individuals bring to the process of staff appraisals and development? The information from the staff appraisals has to be interpreted by those with the experience and knowledge. Receiving appraisal reports from diplomatic missions is not an end in itself, but rather the means to improving performance. Each completed appraisal report contains useful information concerning the strengths and weakness of the respective staff at the diplomatic mission. The information should be used when planning staff training and development programs.

Development diplomacy should not be perceived as a fashion or an exercise in nomenclature. Its introduction means the beginning of change in the way diplomatic missions are managed. There is need to change attitudes and cultures. The concept of time as an adjunct for efficiency must be treated differently for effective interfacing with the private sector. While the public sector has demonstrated the willingness to embrace the new terminology, the private sector is still living in the past. The past in which the government led the way and the private sector followed. That time is gone. And it is counterproductive for the private sector to continue expecting governments to promote trade, investments and tourism without its full involvement. This is the time for the private sector to lead; the leadership which is backed by responsibility and accountability. It is not only the responsibility of offering employment but also contribution to social needs of citizens and promotion of development diplomacy.

John Chikago

<u>REFERENCE:</u>

Torrington.D/Hall .L [1998] – Human Resource Management,
4th Edition, Prentice Hall
Europe, United Kingdom.

Bible – New International Version.

CHAPTER TEN:

INSTITUTIONAL EVALUATION

Ample evidence has been presented on rising public anger for performance improvements at diplomatic missions. This book attempted to explain that such anger is misdirected because diplomatic missions are not independent units. Indeed, governments in developing countries have acted responsibly by implementing development diplomacy as a strategy for improving performance at diplomatic missions.

Naturally, the change has aroused a sense of optimism among citizens by placing their hope in political systems. Isaiah 44:2a says He who made you will help you. This means that hope should be placed in God, the Creator of everything. Warren [2003.p 22] says no person was born by mistake; God plans who will be born and when. In that regard, changing to development diplomacy is not a silver bullet; it cannot realize anything without God's blessing. What are required are prayers asking God for an awakening and awareness to the correct value systems.

Definitely, changing to development diplomacy must be taken as the beginning of a process and not a finite accomplishment. There is need for planning and good decision making. Among other things, there is need to plan for performance measurements that include staff appraisals, job evaluation and benchmarking. These are prerequisites for the success of development diplomacy. The issue is not about nomenclature so as to add confusion to a subject that is already difficult to explain; it is changing strategy for meaningful economic growth in developing countries. While citizens would prefer improvements in the way their diplomatic missions are managed, they also want to know how the existing embassy locations were chosen. Why have embassies here, and not there? Understandably, citizens have the right to know the criteria that is used when selecting mission locations. Their concerns are about cost benefits, or value for money. Their perception equates diplomacy to a commercial activity driven by opportunism.

Consequently, two schools of thought exist: advocating for choosing mission locations based upon environmental factors such as politics, technology, economy and population sizes; the other demanding choices be influenced by resource capabilities. There is no question that both views are correct. What is necessary is to consider how the divergent views can be balanced.

These suggestions seem to ignore the reality on the ground – countries do not have the same numbers of diplomatic missions. Some countries have more diplomatic missions than others; it is not a matter of competition nor is it a matter of economic power. Each country has the freedom to decide on the number of missions after establishing a balance between environmental interests and resource capabilities.

One point to note is that while there are international agreements governing the establishment of diplomatic relations, there is no agreement specifying the correct number of diplomatic missions for any country to operate. It is a subjective choice requiring national consultations and political judgment. In some countries the process of establishing diplomatic missions is rigorous and varies according to historical influences. Regardless of the procedures involved, it is not easy deciding on a magic number considered acceptable. Johnson/Scholes [1999. p 97] warns that the environment encapsulates many different influences; the challenge is on how to make sense from the ever changing situation.

Whether explicit or not, all diplomatic missions are located where they are for a purpose. The purpose could be to promote economic, political and technological interests. The choice to promote is a strategic one, depending upon the development status of the country involved. Some countries aim at casting a wide net by pursuing all strategic opportunities available at a location. In view of budgetary constraints exacerbated by declining terms of trade, the wide net strategy is preferable. Regardless of the range of interests being promoted, it is imperative to monitor performance periodically.

Indeed, the pursuit of development diplomacy has brought forward a wide range of challenges. As a new strategy, there is need to change culture, systems, skills, staff, structures and introduce staff appraisal systems. The previous chapter highlighted why some people do not consider the private sector their first employment choice. The private sector is renowned for using unfair staff appraisal systems, and potential employees are afraid of being victimized. It is not in the interest of public sector management to inherit faulty systems. The introduction of staff appraisal systems has been recommended on condition that proper systems are used.

Comparative Advantages
of Mission Locations

Every mission location has unique opportunities dictating its attractiveness for diplomatic representation. Therefore, before adopting the decision to position an embassy at a specific location, it is important to establish strategic assumptions in terms of the comparative advantages for the operation of a fully fledged diplomatic mission. Once the strategic assumptions have been established and purpose statements prepared, the decision to open a mission can be made.

These will become tools for the evaluation of the mission location. As is the case with any new idea, all diplomatic missions are now expected to promote development diplomacy regardless of the strategic opportunities available at the respective location. This is a strange phenomenon, considering that not all diplomatic locations have the same comparative advantages.

As discussed in preceding chapters, the precondition for the successful implementation of development diplomacy is the preparation of purpose statements, operating objectives, performance targets and job descriptions. The purpose statement would provide the reason for the existence of the respective diplomatic mission at a particular location. Without the purpose statement, it would be practically impossible to evaluate the performance of mission locations.

The scriptures are clear when it comes to the management of change. Mark 2:21-22 warns against pouring new wine into old wine skins. Therefore, before expecting too much from the change to development diplomacy, it is necessary to review the strategic opportunities available at all mission locations. The reviews will help to show if the original opportunities still exist at each of the mission locations. The disadvantage of strategic opportunities is their vulnerability to political situations, social conditions, economic growth and technological advances.

A good example is the former countries of Eastern Europe, which previously gave development aid to poor countries. Now those same countries cannot afford to contribute any form of aid. These changing trends in the global village reinforce the need for continuous evaluation of mission locations to ensure conformity to original purposes.

Evidence of divergence from original purposes and strategic assumptions is a cause for serious concern. An immediate investigation should follow with the aim of reviewing the extent of the disparity. Results of the study should also be useful for resource planning.

At times, it is easier for bureaucrats to conduct arbitrary evaluations with preconceived intentions of denigrating others for lack of contributions. It must be appreciated that strategic situations are influenced by many factors such as geopolitical environmental changes. Therefore, it is wrong to undertake performance evaluations of mission locations hastily. Evaluations must follow strategic considerations to avoid making wrong decisions.

This does not mean relocating a diplomatic mission is a mistake. When evidence reveals shifting strategic opportunities, it is unpatriotic not to relocate to better places.

Even the scriptures support the need to cut trees which do not bear fruits. Matthew 21:18-19 explains the spiritual view of good fruits; a tree that does not produce fruit should be cut down, regardless of its leaves. It is important that any decision to relocate should be made after reviewing the initial reasons for choosing the particular location. The agenda to realize national economic growth through development diplomacy requires selflessness and strategic thinking.

Benchmarking

Benchmarking seeks to assess the competence of an organization against the best in the industry wherever found. It is sometimes known as inter-firm comparison. Johnson/Scholes [2003.p181] advises that benchmarking begins in a simple way. However, it has emerged as a powerful technique in recent years for evaluating organizations operating in similar businesses. This is not to say that every good thing originates from the private sector; the tendency of using unfair staff appraisal systems has already been highlighted. In the interest of time and money, it is convenient to use benchmarking as a performance evaluation system.

The practice has been used for many years by United Kingdom firms competing for business. For example, a commercial bank would compare its performance against a competitor to see where it needs to improve. Similarly, a transport company would compare its fuel consumption records with its competitor. Since the objective is to improve performance, comparisons are useful as barometers of poor performance. Obviously, comparisons of this nature require the development of friendship and trust. In fact, it is a confidence building measure. Managers who agree to subject their businesses to such comparisons cannot be enemies.

The practice is similar to the peer review mechanism touted as the magic medicine for the entrenchment of democratic governance in Africa through the New Partnership for Africa's Development [NEPAD]. Yes, it is a good long-term strategy when perceived as a cultural process with a starting point, but without an end point. Good systems tend to suffer from inherent subjectivities. Without the carrot and stick, the possibility exists that peer pressure will become additional terminology fodder for students of political science. However, there is no harm in trying to do better than before; that is how progress is made. African leaders deserve commendation for the courage and vision.

The benchmarking technique can also be a valuable tool for the evaluation of diplomatic institutions. Apart from conducting the strategic performance tests suggested in preceding paragraphs, it is advisable to compare one mission against another at the same location. Similarly, the comparisons could be extended to missions from the same country on the control of specific variable costs. This approach would help to expose performance on an equal basis.

It has to be accepted that performance is a combination of many things, such as resources and environmental trends. Nevertheless, it is unwise to perceive diplomatic missions as commercial enterprises. Their contributions have a cyclic trend.

Institutional evaluation provides useful comparative information, on condition that it is used properly. Concern has already been raised about misuse of such information to mete punishments on subordinate employees. Job evaluations provide information on job content to ensure that not all jobs are rated equally. Institutional evaluation is necessary for ensuring periodic reviews of original mandates against changes to environmental assumptions.

The Principle of Reciprocity

The practice of diplomacy has principles. One of the principles is that of reciprocity. Ideally, the starting point for any vibrant bilateral relationship is the exchange of diplomatic representatives. Without the exchange of diplomatic representatives, it is correct to conclude that the relations are not very friendly. For this reason, countries have to evaluate the strategic importance of friendly states on the basis of resident ambassadors. When the relationship is heart to heart, the bilateral relations will translate into the exchange of resident ambassadors.

In practical terms, there is no substitute for the exchange of resident ambassadors. Maintenance of embassies and staff remunerations create a steady inflow of foreign currencies, indirectly helping the growth of the economy in the host country. Non-resident diplomats only help to promote tourism incomes during their periodic visits. This is an important point when evaluating the value of diplomatic relations. Unfortunately, the local presence of diplomatic staffs is usually not perceived from the context of economic contributions.

The implication is that when two developing countries exchange resident ambassadors they are actually exchanging financial sacrifices. It costs money to look after diplomatic staffs in foreign countries. The embassy needs water, electricity, stationery, motor vehicles and fuel. Apart from these amenities, there is the practice of engaging support staff from the host country. Their remunerations are received in foreign currencies, which maybe the cause foreign exchange inflation in the economy of the sending state. This is the paradox that is resolved through the reciprocity of diplomatic representation.

John Chikago

REFERENCES:

Johnson. G/Scholes. K[1999.p181] – Exploring Corporate Strategy, 5th Edition, Prentice Hall, England.

Warren.R [2003] – The Purpose Driven Life Purpose-Driven Ministries, Philippines.

Bible – New International Version

ABOUT THE AUTHOR

John Chikago is the Ambassador of the Republic of Malawi to Japan. He is a specialist in organizations and management. He has a track record for turning ailing organizations to effective performance.

He is a born again Christian; believing that no country can realize any economic development without placing faith in God. The faith must be steadfast; not the type that wavers from time to time like a ship in high seas.

He calls himself a man of two worlds; combining 23 years of private sector experience; involving the production of beer, furniture, ladies wear and tea manufacture with diplomacy. He believes the background has enabled him to author this book.

He describes Japan as a huge open university where personal traits for creativity and consciousness are reinvigorated. When asked about his mission to Japan, his answer is simple and straight-forward; to promote the Republic of Malawi as the preferred trade, tourism and investment destination for Japanese. Ambassador Chikago is the author of another book entitled CROSSING CULTURAL FRONTIERS aimed at deepening cross-cultural understanding between Japanese and Malawians.

He says the purpose of his books is to create a new way of thinking in developing countries. He believes that solutions to old problems cannot come from old thinking. The new thinking requires new ethics. And the correct ethics are in the Holy Bible. As a born-again Christian, he believes that the implementation of development diplomacy will not realize anything without placing faith in God. He says the book is his ministry to believers in developing countries of the world.

Apart from his rich private sector experience, Ambassador Chikago holds a number of professional qualifications including MBA degree in public sector management from the Buckinghamshire Chilterns University College, in the United Kingdom.

He loves watching television, reading and writing during his leisure time.

www.ingramcontent.com/pod-product-compliance
Lightning Source LLC
Chambersburg PA
CBHW020415290526
45785CB00002B/570